TEACHING INTRODUCTORY
PSYCHOLOGY

TEACHING INTRODUCTORY PSYCHOLOGY

ROZ BRODY & NICKY HAYES

LAWRENCE ERLBAUM ASSOCIATES, PUBLISHERS
Hove (UK)   Hillsdale (USA)

Lawrence Erlbaum Associates Ltd., Publishers
27 Church Road
Hove
East Sussex
BN3 2FA, UK

British Library Cataloguing in Publication Data

A catalogue record for this book is available from the British Library

ISBN 0-86377-373-7

Cartoons by Sanz
Cover design by Joyce Chester
Printed and bound by Redwood Books, Trowbridge, Wiltshire

Contents

1

General introduction

ABOUT THIS BOOK

"Teaching Introductory Psychology" has been written to help both new and experienced teachers and lecturers to use the "Principles of Psychology" series to teach psychology courses. "Teaching Introductory Psychology" attempts to provide the teacher with ideas and practical help in their teaching.

This book provides:

- Some ideas for how teaching can be structured, and for topic sequences during a modular course.

- Discussions of the major themes and issues which emerge in, or can be drawn from, the different topics.

- Topic-by-topic ideas for how to help to bring the subject alive for students in the classroom, or in a seminar group, together with comments and suggestions about how students sometimes react to different topics.

- Ideas for practical work.

- Sets of key terms and names of significant psychologists.

- Suggestions for essay and revision questions.

In this book, we have tried to present some of our own ideas for making psychology teaching a useful and enjoyable experience. We have always found that teaching psychology is fun, and we hope that you will too. We hope also that this book will help you to make the most of the "Principles of Psychology" series or of any other course texts which you may be using.

HOW TO USE THE "PRINCIPLES" SERIES

Although this book can be used as a teaching companion with most introductory psychology textbooks, it has been particularly designed to coordinate with the Erlbaum "Principles of Psychology" series. The "Principles of Psychology" series was initially designed for A and AS level students, though each of the modules has relevance and usefulness for other courses too. The diagram overleaf shows how the different modules may be related in a typical introductory psychology course.

The "Perspectives" module is central, in that it both integrates and draws from all of the other modules. The other texts provide a comprehensive coverage of relevant areas. Each of them is a free-standing text in its own right, and so may be used either independently or in combination with one another, as desired.

The order in which a lecturer teaches the modules is largely a matter of personal choice.

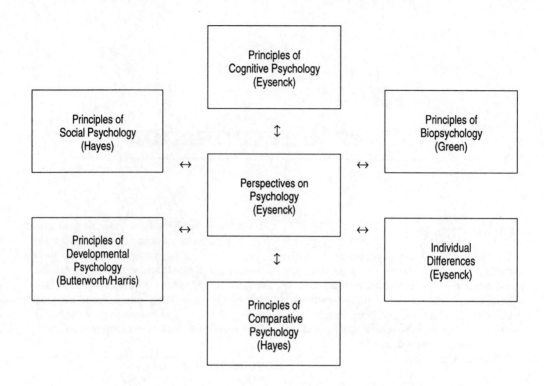

Some lecturers prefer to start with topics which relate most closely to what their students are already aware of in their personal experience, while others prefer to deal with less overtly conscious topics first, such as physiological psychology, and only move to more familiar areas once they are sure that students have become familiar with the demands of psychological analysis.

Whether you begin or end your course with "Perspectives" is up to you. Some teachers like to establish the main themes as groundwork beforehand, others like to use the themes to draw together and re-evaluate what has been learned at the end of the course. There is no single right answer, and in any case, "Perspectives" can be highlighted throughout the teaching of the various topics as well.

Roz Brody & Nicky Hayes

The "Principles of Psychology" series consists of the following texts:

- Perspectives on Psychology, Michael W. Eysenck

- Principles of Cognitive Psychology, Michael W. Eysenck

- Principles of Social Psychology, Nicky Hayes

- Principles of Developmental Psychology, George Butterworth & Margaret Harris

- Individual Differences, Michael W. Eysenck

- Principles of Biopsychology, Simon Green

- Principles of Comparative Psychology, Nicky Hayes

2

Key aims and principles

INTRODUCTION

This chapter is all about the woods and forests which we see when we raise our heads from examination of the trees and leaves of psychological knowledge. In it, we discuss the overarching issues and principles which arise when one is teaching the different aspects of introductory psychology. Psychological topics are interesting in their own right, but they are also invaluable for introducing students to different types of debate, different types of theory, and the different types of research methodology found in modern and historical psychology.

The study of any psychological topic raises educational issues about what we are actually trying to communicate to our students, and why that particular topic has been deemed a suitable part of an introductory syllabus. Nature–nurture, for instance, is hardly a "hot" research topic for psychologists, but it appears on introductory syllabuses because it provides a manageable introduction to the nature–nurture question, and allows students to bring different forms of research evidence together into an appropriate synthesis. It is a useful teaching tool for introducing a more general issue which has influenced many different branches of psychology.

The ultimate purpose of this chapter, then, is to look at why we are studying particular aspects of psychology, and what general principles we can draw out from them. We have also discussed many of the debates between differing schools of thought which arise from those general principles, and given some illustrations of how particular issues might be raised or highlighted with students.

PERSPECTIVES ON PSYCHOLOGY

Introduction
Students often find "Perspectives" the most challenging area in the whole of psychology. There are several reasons for this, not least of which is the way that it requires them to have a higher overview of the discipline, and to engage in an appraisal of knowledge which is different from the other subjects they are likely to have encountered. Furthermore, the differing views about what psychology is, what psychologists should study and how they should go about studying it often results in students begging to know "but who is *right*?".

It may be difficult for students to apprehend at first, but in the end, tackling "Perspectives" is probably one of the most educational experiences they are likely to encounter. This is because it introduces students to important epistemological issues, and, most importantly, to the way that our philosophical definitions of the world and

THE SEARCH FOR A UNIFIED APPROACH TO PSYCHOLOGY CONTINUES...

what counts as important can determine just about everything we experience.

Perhaps the most important issue to get across here is that these perspectives are not simply abstract concepts, with no direct relevance to the topics being studied. They permeate all areas of psychology, and it is important to help students understand how the current controversies within psychology have their roots in its historical development.

Indeed, the key issue of the relationship between body and mind/soul has a habit of returning and informing debates about reductionism, free will, and determinism. Plato's hierarchical division of the soul into three elements, with rational thought and intelligence at the top, raises a number of issues about the link between rational and emotional behaviour, and indeed about why rational thought is given higher status than emotional experience. The division can be

linked to Freud's distinction between the id, ego and superego, or to the various theories of emotion, or even, at a pinch, to the physiological distinction between the hind-, mid- and forebrain.

In much the same way, Aristotle's laws of association, contiguity, similarity and contrast can be linked both to behaviourist theories, and to research into memory. The suggestion made by the 17th-century philosopher, David Hartley, that there is a physiological basis to the association of ideas can be linked to the various debates about localisation and modularity of function in the brain, as can Descartes' search for the soul. Descartes can also be used to discuss both the similarities and differences between animals and humans, and Spinoza's double aspect theory can be used to debate the difference between physiological and psychological explanations. Although students often find it disheartening that their insights were debated by philosophers centuries ago, the connections between these early ideas and various themes and issues in psychology say something important about the continuous and socially-located nature of knowledge.

Current approaches & historical roots

For many students, the contrasting approaches to psychology can be confusing rather than enlightening. Despite many approaches sharing the same pioneers, such as Darwin, it is clear that behaviourists, psychoanalysts, psychometricians and ethologists have all chosen to colonise different areas of human activity. There is often very little consistency between one area and the next in terms of fundamental assumptions, methods of study and ideas of what constitutes an adequate explanation.

The important issue to emphasise here is the idea of *levels of explanation*. We can't hope to explain everything that human beings do by looking at it from just one angle. Instead, we need to look at human activity from several perspectives: understanding why someone becomes enraged when the top has been left off the tube of toothpaste for the 53rd time may have a social component (irritation with family members), a behavioural component (familiar habits), a physiological component (arousal level), and several more. No single level of explanation is enough to explain it, but together they can all contribute to our understanding of what is going on. It is important to stress that the different approaches often have different aims: a useful contrast being the humanists' emphasis on understanding and self-growth, and the behaviourists' stress on prediction and control.

In addition, the diversity of approaches and interests allows students to explore some of the key issues within psychology, many of which revolve around the status of psychology as a science and the debates surrounding the artificiality of lab studies and the limitation of scientific method. Other concerns revolve around whether psychology is essentially limited to the study of human beings, or whether it can realistically branch out to other species; and if so, to what extent.

The different approaches can be pulled together by focusing on a particular area such as abnormal psychology, for in this domain behaviourists, humanists, psychoanalysts, biopsychologists, cognitive psychologists, and social and developmental psychologists all share an interest.

It is also important to emphasise to students that the different areas which are outlined here are not homogeneous. Within each approach there is diversity, as can be seen in the differences between the American and European schools of social psychology, or in differences between the individually-oriented psychoanalytic theory put forward by Freud, or the more socially-oriented theory put forward by later psychoanalysts such as Fromm. There are similar contrasts and divergences of approach in each of the areas.

Major issues in psychology

Underlying the major issues in psychology is the key question of how we see human beings. Are we unique individuals, as the idiographic approach implies, or are we to be understood better by searching for general laws, as the nomothetic approach suggests? Can all human behaviour be explained in terms of biochemistry, S-R connections or computer analogies, or are some types of explanation more suited to some types of behaviour?

The issue of reductionism also allows discussion of the status given to some forms of explanation over others. Once again, areas in abnormal psychology can be used to help students to see how different explanations can contribute to our understanding. A good example is schizophrenia, where research on dopamine can be compared with the research undertaken on family life or cross-cultural studies.

Free will and determination might be explored by looking at social, individual and genetic beliefs about the nature of criminality or aggression. Another possibility is to look at Tourette's syndrome, in which the person's use of expletives is perceived as being outside their control.

You might want to try and link the idiographic and nomothetic approach by looking at the nature of science and suggesting that the idiographic approach contributes to both description and understanding whilst the nomothetic approach emphasises prediction and control. A third dimension which is worth bringing in here is the hermeneutic approach, which emphasises meaning in social experience. Many of the more recent developments in psychology, such as social cognition, are based on this type of approach rather than a straightforward idiographic/nomothetic distinction.

It is important for students to consider the ethical and practical implications of research findings relating to nature–nurture debates. Above all, the debates need to be located within their socio-political contexts, since they are central to understanding why the issue has become so important.

The nature–nurture debate also allows you to explore some of the implications of advances in technology, with respect to genetic engineering and the social consequences of the Human Genome Project.

Finally, explorations of different types of consciousness allow you to raise questions about the nature of awareness, and of levels of mind. These concepts can also be linked with questions about evolution, and/or about psychology itself.

Motivation and emotion

At first sight it might seem that motivation lies at the heart of psychology, since it refers to the "why" of human behaviour. Students rapidly learn, however, that conventional psychological coverage of the term "motivation" is far more limited. One important principle to bear in mind, therefore, is the existence of a diverse range of human motives. These span social and cultural motives as well as cognitive and physiological ones.

One issue which comes up relatively quickly is the way that using motives as an explanation is fraught with problems. It is often worth taking a historical approach to this: encouraging students first to explore the concept of drives, including ideas about primary and secondary drives, before going on to discuss the weaknesses of the drive approach and alternative ways of conceptualising motivation (internal/external motives etc.).

A historical perspective can also help to illuminate some of the differences in psychological emphasis. Earlier research tended to focus on physiological needs, and used animals, while later research tended to focus more on cognitive factors, and hence used humans. This also raises the question of the next wave of research, and the likely recognition of social factors in motivation, which in turn can lead into a consideration of how psychological research reflects the interests and concerns of its wider society.

The psychological study of emotions also raises a number of questions. Some of the obvious difficulties are attempts to produce general definitions of the structure of emotions. For example, while there is some agreement that there are five components of emotional responses: cognitive, physiological, experiential, expressive and behavioural, as far as psychological research is concerned there seems to be a distinct lack of concordance between them.

The mind–body link returns to haunt the topic with both James–Lange and Cannon–Bard's theories. There are also a number of questions to be raised about labelling theory—not least of which is the idea of whether labelling might or might not be a factor in emotional experience, even if, as is apparent from the evidence, it is not the only explanation.

Research into the cognitive labelling of emotions clearly raises ethical issues as participants were invariably deceived—and in some cases, powerful soporific drugs (chlorpromazine) were administered without their knowledge.

The study of both emotions and motives forces students to contemplate the most appropriate methodology to use when trying to study them, and this area can allow students to see some of the benefits of using case studies to evaluate theories.

Finally, one of the most important points to encourage students to consider is why research into emotions has concentrated so much on the darker side of human nature, and why positive emotions have generated very little research. Again, this leads into questions about scientific research in its social context.

Research methods

Any discussion of research methods will raise the emphasis given to scientific method and the aim of the psychological discipline to establish psychology as a science. But this, in turn, leads to considerations of what actually constitutes a science. Freud, for example, believed that his approach was scientific in that his theories were strictly based on the evidence which he was obtaining from his patients. However, concepts of science have changed considerably in the past century, and the combination of qualitative description and the non-materialistic notion of "psychological truth" in Freud's theories resulted in his work being seen as unscientific.

Considering issues like this can also lead to a discussion of methods. It is often assumed, for instance, that the use of case studies was a weakness in Freud's work, and yet case studies have always been extensively used in neuropsychology and cognitive psychology without resulting in either of those areas being regarded as unscientific.

Introducing research methods leads to consideration of how the advantages of one approach to research constitute the disadvantages of another approach. The behaviourist emphasis on operational definitions, prediction and control led to criticisms of triviality and ethical malpractice, whilst the humanists' anti-scientific stance resulted in humanism being perceived as a fringe area of psychology during the 1960s and 1970s.

It is also worthwhile to get students to consider whether we can ever establish causal relationships, or whether we are doomed to infer them. This raises the issue of the ecological validity of isolating one variable to see the effect it has on the dependent variable, when in everyday life more than one variable is in operation at any one time.

It is also important to consider the problems of demand characteristics, experimenter bias, evaluation apprehension and the difficulties of sampling. This can be linked with the ethical expectation of respect for research participants, and the concomitant shift away from the old manipulative mind-set. In turn, this raises the question of whether less tightly controlled methods of research, such as action research and interviewing, will actually provide more valid data and lead to more valuable theories.

The relationship between theory and data is also interesting to explore in the light of paradigm shifts and how such shifts occur. Kuhn's idea that psychology was in a pre-scientific stage because it lacked a dominant paradigm can be discussed (although it is questionable how far this idea was actually based on a knowledge of psychology at the time, since behaviourism was quite dominant as a paradigm). Alternatively, paradigm shifts in psychology can be introduced by inviting students to consider the shift from introspectionism, to behaviourism, and then to the cognitive revolution.

You might also invite students to consider Popper's concept of refutation and falsification as an important feature of scientific endeavour. Is it really possible, for instance, to refute cognitive flow-charts of mental processes? Why do we consider them to be scientific while Freud's theories are not?

Students might also like to consider why some articles get published in journals rather than others, and why some areas of research are extensively funded, while others are not. Why, for example, has there been extensive research into sleep deprivation, in which people have gone without sleep for days on end, yet very little research into the effects of the kind of restricted, interrupted sleep suffered by parents of very young children?

The conduct of research
Perhaps the hardest problem which students face when they are really trying to get their teeth into ethical issues is the fact that there are no easy answers or absolute rules.

The British Psychological Society's ethical guidelines focus on issues such as informed consent, confidentiality, the use and abuse of deception and the right of participants to withdraw both themselves and their data. These, clearly, betoken a radical shift in attitude towards the research participants, and you might like to encourage students to consider what this shift actually implies for psychology in the future.

Students might also like to contemplate its implications for the past: how Milgram or Asch could have run their studies without using deception, given the way that phrases like "don't worry, he's not really getting an electric shock", or "I'm trying to see if you go along

"MAKE A NOTE, SMALLWICK; 'DAY ONE:- SUBJECT EXHIBITED MILD ANXIETY SYNDROME.'"

with group consensus" would have markedly altered the findings.

The rise in concerns about ethical issues over the past couple of decades makes it particularly important that students should be encouraged to see psychological knowledge in a historical context. Studies which appeared perfectly acceptable in the 1960s would not be permissible now, and it is important to emphasise how students need to bear that, and the ethical guidelines, in mind when planning their own practical work.

The practical applications of research in such areas as token economy and aversion therapy raise issues over who decides whether we should change other people's behaviour, as well as the age-old debate over who controls the controllers.

Animal research also raises questions about whether the search for knowledge justifies some of the methodologies used, and if so, how far this argument can be taken. While some students will inevitably see this as having a straightforward, simple and absolute answer, it is important to emphasise that ethical decisions are almost always a question of balancing up different demands.

Finally, as well as looking at the ethical implications of methods of research, it is important that students should consider how psychological theories and findings are actually used, and indeed, whether research findings should be published at all if they could be used to support racist ideologies. This raises the question of social responsibility of science, and the wider ethical concerns which arise because psychology exists in society, rather than in a vacuum.

COGNITIVE PSYCHOLOGY

What is cognitive psychology?

There are a number of themes and issues which emerge from the study of cognitive psychology, and which can be usefully drawn out when teaching it. One of them, which permeates almost all aspects of cognitive psychology, is the top-down/bottom-up issue. Top-down theories are those which begin from a very general starting point, which is assumed to influence how all the basic underlying processes take place. So they express some generative principle and then show how the details of the topic conform or follow logically from that principle. Bottom-up theories, on the other hand, adopt a "jigsaw-puzzle" approach, trying to piece together cognitive processes by studying the fine detail of components, and building them up into a more general picture. There are theories representing each of these approaches in almost every area of cognitive psychology.

Another issue which permeates many topics in modern cognitive psychology is the computer metaphor: the idea that the human brain somehow functions "like" a computer. There are many critics of cognitive psychology who feel that this metaphor has been taken too far, and that it has distracted attention from other, more "human" aspects of cognitive psychology.

An essential message to communicate to students who are looking at human cognitive psychology is that cognition is not simply about mechanical recording. Instead, cognitive processes involve interpretation, modification, understanding etc., and any model which is developed to account for cognitive processes needs to be able to account for this.

Sensory systems & perception

This area can be broken down into four different components of human perception: how sensory systems work, perceptual development, perceptual organisation, and theories of perception. There are a number of messages here, but perhaps the most important one to communicate to students is that you need to look at any given aspect of human experience from more than one angle in order to understand it.

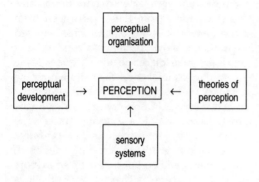

Another theme which may be useful to highlight in this area is that of the range of different methodological techniques which have been used in studies of perception. Although largely within the experimental psychology tradition, these range from the mainly introspective studies of the Gestalt psychologists to tightly controlled laboratory studies requiring extremely sophisticated equipment.

Many themes and perspectives are apparent in this topic, and can be used to encourage students to develop their ability to take a broad overview of an area. Some of the most readily apparent are: ethical issues and animal research, the question of reductionism, the nature–nurture debate, and the development and application of top-down or bottom-up theories of perception. It is also possible to link areas of research in this module with other modules, such as developmental psychology.

Attention

Attention is generally a fairly straightforward topic to teach, and one which allows you to provide students with examples of a number of general issues. One of these is that it is able to address questions about the use of models

as aids to understanding what is going on. The development of filter models in response to experimental data gives a particularly clear example of the relationship between theory and experiment, and the cyclical process of refining theories in response to new empirical data.

It is useful to point out to students that the word "attention" is ambiguous, and is used in the literature with at least three different meanings. Sometimes it is used to talk about attention being selective in the sense of noticing some things and not others. Sometimes the concept is used like a spotlight, with attention being focused on some things particularly and not others, and therefore allows you to discuss automatic routines and tasks which don't require concentration. Sometimes, too, it is used as if it were synonymous with concentrating: "I just can't take that in: I can't possibly attend to it any more".

This triple use of the term is reflected in the structure of the field of study. Some research into attention is concerned with selective attention and the way that we ignore some things but notice others; other aspects of research are concerned with divided attention, stressing how many things can be done at once, and often emphasising the role of practice, experts and novices, and task and response similarity. Other research, particularly that concerning vigilance, is concerned with how long and under what circumstances we can keep on attending to things.

One of the themes which also emerges from the study of attention is that of the real-life application of research. The military application of vigilance studies and research into selective attention may be used to raise questions about the relationship between research funding and theoretical development, as well as broader issues. The way in which technological development permitted the investigation of areas previously accessible only through introspective techniques may also raise questions about the relationship between the nature of scientific knowledge and the real world.

Memory

Perhaps the most important message in this topic is the idea that memory is not a tape-recording: that the information which we remember is not a simple factual account of what happened. Although this issue tends to become lost or taken for granted when looking at storage models and other recent theories of memory processing, it is one which is intuitively obvious, and so it needs emphasising in the classroom or seminar group.

It is also important to stress that the way information is processed influences how much we can remember. The central principle to get across is the idea that we remember things that we have elaborated, modified or in other senses processed. However, as a general rule, we do not remember those things that we have not processed. This concept is implicit in other theories as well as the levels of processing approach, and since it raises the idea that it is possible to exert some personal control over one's memory, it is an important one.

Following on from this, and raised naturally by it, is the idea that there are also other ways that information gets into memory, since some of the information that we remember seems to be acquired involuntarily and without effort, e.g. advertising slogans and other trivia. Theories of flashbulb memory, unconscious processing etc. may help to provide a framework for these questions.

This topic also raises the age-old problem faced by psychologists: how do we know what is going on inside someone's head? In many

"WHAT BOTHERS ME, IS HOW WILL I KNOW WHEN I *HAVE* FORGOTTEN EVERYTHING?"

models of memory, boxes and circles tend to replace grey matter, and this can be used to raise questions about the use of analogies and metaphors in theory-building.

Language comprehension & production

This topic is a particularly fruitful one for focusing on the top-down/bottom-up debate. Early models of language, such as those which emphasised transformational grammar or other "componential" approaches to understanding language provide clear examples of bottom-up processing; whereas the more recent approaches which emphasise the social dimensions of plans, goals and scripts in understanding language represent very clear examples of top-down processing.

Since the present focus is to move away from grammar to focus on semantics and context—specifically the social context—this can also be used to discuss whether there is a growing paradigm shift in psychology which emphasises the role of social factors in cognitive processes a great deal more. Students may be encouraged to look at the evidence for the idea that all cognitive processes are affected by social factors; and to contrast it with (a) more conventional approaches implicit in current research, and (b) the computer metaphor.

Another valuable angle which can be drawn out of this topic is the range of methodology involved in the psychological study of any real aspects of human experience. The various methods of study which have been applied to the study of language range from rigidly controlled laboratory experiments to discourse analysis, case studies and many other approaches. So, the topic as a whole can be seen as a microcosm of the range of psychological methods. It may also be useful to contrast the methods used in this area with those used in an area of cognitive psychology which draws more strongly from the experimental tradition, such as perception or memory.

Thinking

This topic naturally raises questions about what thinking really is, and how far psychological research has adequately defined and studied it. Discussion of this issue can be used to articulate the essential differences between reasoning, problem solving, concept formation, judgements and decision making, as topics which are included in conventional psychological research, and also aspects of other types of thinking, such as day-dreaming or fantasy, which are not.

Research into thinking also raises some very clear questions about the relevance and applicability of the computer metaphor in cognitive psychology, since it is here that recent research shows the influence of this metaphor most strongly. Consequently, it raises issues about the similarities and, perhaps more importantly, the differences, between computers and humans. Humans often come off worse in terms of rational thinking, storage, and so on, but this is often seen as a consequence of an extremely narrow definition of the problem, and a refusal to acknowledge the broader social and probabilistic knowledge which human beings apply in problem solving, and which is not available for computers.

These features of human thinking also become apparent in research into decision making and judgement. The end result of the extensive application of the computer metaphor in research into thinking, however, is that it produces a perceptual set in which human thinking is primarily seen as being about "errors", rather than being about applying a sophisticated and complex world-knowledge. In this context, there is much fruitful material which can be used to direct students' attention towards a potential paradigm shift which emphasises the social contexts and functions of cognition rather than seeing it as a series of individualised, acontextual processes.

SOCIAL PSYCHOLOGY

The contexts of social interaction

The starting point for teaching social psychology needs to stress that social interaction always takes place within a social, physical, cultural and historical context. Even that most elusive construct, the self-concept, has been socially constructed, and is dependent on the cultural context within which it is located.

Given this, the relevance of laboratory studies becomes a key issue within social psychology. While such research might reveal how people behave in psychology experiments, and how science and power influence people, they don't necessarily help us to understand everyday life. Other types of research also raise questions. Are observational psychologists merely voyeurs? Why should people bother to answer questionnaires truthfully?

As well as raising problems with appropriate methodology, this module allows students to explore paradigm shifts. In particular, psychologists are beginning to look at how people account for their own behaviour, letting them speak for themselves, rather than speaking on their behalf. This inevitably links with the new emphasis on ethical responsibility in psychology.

Finally, social psychology should allow you to introduce ideas about power, roles, scripts and schemas in everyday living. Get the students to think about what can go wrong in human interaction, and to explore the importance of shared world views and cultural perspectives to how we go about interacting with other people.

Conversation & communication

Students invariably enjoy learning about non-verbal communication, in that this is what they think psychology should be all about: being able to look at people and know what they are thinking by whether their arms are folded or not, and so on. For this reason, it is important to emphasise that psychologists haven't got all the answers!

Nonetheless, discussion of social communication can provide students with genuine insight into how people interact. One area that can be explored is the function of non-verbal communication, given that human beings can both say and write down what they feel. You might discuss how we gain our knowledge and understanding of social interaction, since it is not part of the National Curriculum. This could link with developmental or comparative psychology.

You can also use this area to discuss some of the applications of psychological research. Should people be given courses on "how to make friends and influence people"? Should politicians be given courses on how to get votes? Is it possible to draw a line between enhancement of social skills and manipulating others?

Discussions of attribution theory can often result in students wanting to challenge psychological assumptions about how human beings function. It raises the issue of whether psychologists are trying to get human beings to fit theoretical models that don't necessarily describe what is really going on, when we try to explain someone else's behaviour. It raises the age-old question of "how do we know?" and brings us back to methodology and interpretation.

Recent work on discourse analysis and social representations provides a clear illustration of the paradigm shift taking place within social psychology, both in the methods used to investigate these phenomena, and in the choice of subject itself. You might like to contrast these aspects of modern social psychology with older, more established areas like NVC or conformity, perhaps linking it with broader perspectives such as the influence of behaviourism and the cognitive revolution.

Interacting with others

This is a key area within social psychology, raising questions about who influences us, how they influence us, and why they influence us.

The studies done on conformity, obedience and bystander intervention immediately raise issues about ethics and whether the means justifies the end. These topics can be used to discuss difficulties with research methodology. Milgram couldn't have told his participants the aim of the study without affecting them. Does that justify the use of deception? Predictions as to the possible outcomes of his studies were wildly inaccurate: his findings were counter-intuitive, telling us something we didn't know about people. Does that affect how we should judge the deception?

It is also important to raise the wider aspects of human society, and to look at psychological knowledge in its social context. Historical factors, which are often omitted from social psychology, might be explored in the light of different eras. For example: were the Sixties more likely to encourage non-conformist behaviour?

The link to everyday life is crucial for helping students to understand some of the key issues. Unfortunately numerous examples from the real world can be used to explore topics like obedience and conformity (e.g. Nazi Germany). There are some positive ones too: the more positive aspects of bystander intervention studies, or recent findings about rebellion and minority influence. Linking research back to the real world allows students to discuss whether the aim of psychology is merely to describe, explain and understand people, or whether the psychologists' role is to use their knowledge to change or improve human behaviour. And how far does the latter lead to a "Brave New World" approach?

Finally, it is worthwhile to explore the reasons why some people are less likely to be influenced by other people and why some will stand alone. This can lead to discussions of social identity, self-concept and individual differences.

Person perception, attraction & relationships

A good opener to this area might be to stress that how we see ourselves plays a key role in how we perceive other people, which can be used to emphasise the interactive aspects of person perception. It also allows students to examine the power base within society by discussing which groups of people are more likely to be stereotyped and why.

Ethical discussions are likely to come to the fore when examining research on attractiveness and attraction, and these studies can provide some very clear examples of the more manipulative aspects of social psychological research. It also allows you to raise broader issues like ethnocentricity in psychology: is it all based on the dating behaviour of the lesser-spotted North American Undergraduate?

Indeed, the whole area of human relationships can be seen as an exceptionally difficult area to research, which might help to explain why some of the earlier research tended to focus on fairly trivial aspects of human relationships. While the earlier studies tended to see the individuals within relationships as static commodities who could be compared in terms of similarities and differences, more recent research focuses on the nature of relationships: how they develop and are maintained as well as looking at why they break down.

The contrasting methodologies involved in the two types of research might be linked to the broader paradigm shift taking place within social psychology. The different theoretical models of relationships can also be analysed in terms of this shift, or alternatively as raising issues of reductionism, or of cultural values in psychology. For example, discussions of social exchange theory allow students to explore whether economic analogies are relevant to human beings, as well as discussing whether people are really as calculating as some psychologists have suggested. This can be contrasted with the process and cognitive similarity models of relationships.

Attitudes

It is easy to get bogged down in this area, particularly when dealing with the distinction between attitudes and opinions and the relationship between the cognitive, conative and behavioural dimensions. It's probably easiest to begin by asking questions like: what is the point of attitudes? Do they tell us anything about people? And how do they relate to other aspects of people's world-views?

Methodological issues might be explored by looking at how we actually measure attitudes. This can be used to raise a number of questions about reliability and validity, including whether people would answer the questions truthfully; bringing in discussions of real-life measures of attitudes, such as opinion polls during election time or marketing research. Again, the influence of behaviourism on methodology can be explored, and contrasted with the different methodologies involved in more modern areas of social psychology.

The differences between expressed attitudes and observable behaviour are a perennial theme, and you might use it to raise

CERTAIN ASPECTS OF THE QUESTIONNAIRE TRIED GAVIN'S CAPACITY FOR HONESTY.

the issue of whether people are even aware of what their attitudes are. This might bring in Bem's self-perception theory: do we know ourselves better from our behaviour rather than from our subjective feelings? It might also bring in issues of social identification: how far does belonging to a social group bring with it an obligation to act in a particular way?

Persuasion allows you to discuss the role of psychologist as manipulator. Should we try to change people's attitudes and behaviour? The use of propaganda can also be used to emphasise the power of the media and its ability to provide people with frameworks for understanding the world in which they live, and this can be linked with social representation theory. But, of course, the most important application here is advertising: it is worth scrutinising each of the theories and concepts in this area in terms of how they have been applied in the advertising world.

On a higher-order level, it can be argued that the reason why there have been relatively few developments in attitude research over the past 30 years is because (a) it has been superseded by more relevant concepts like attribution or social representations; (b) it is dependent on an information-processing model of the human being, no longer regarded as adequate, or (c) all of the psychologists involved in the field have found it more lucrative to go and work in advertising than to do academic research. You may like to get students to discuss these questions, but probably separately.

Conflict & co-operation

This topic allows you to bring some insight to the nastier excesses of human behaviour, but it also raises a number of higher order questions, like why have psychologists spent so much time studying aggression, and so little on co-operation? How does that reflect Western society's own obsessions (e.g. news,

TV programme content, etc.)? One valuable question is to ask: how come, if human beings are so nasty, they live together in social groups at all? Links with comparative psychology suggest that such behaviour is not usually found in highly social animals, but with more isolated species. A time-perspective may show a link with social representation theory: how do the different interests of psychologists reflect what else was going on in society at the time? And what are the political uses of theories portraying the darker side of human nature?

Biological vs. social perspectives on aggression are important themes in this respect, as is distinguishing between different types of aggressive behaviour. What is the difference between shoving someone aside in a queue, murdering your partner after years of abuse, or shooting a young child because you are a soldier and following orders? You may like to link this with research into conformity, obedience and rebellion.

On the more positive side, research into altruism reveals that humans don't always act out of self-interest, even though some students will find biological theories of altruism appealing (sic). Similarly, the old "mob" theories of crowd behaviour may be contrasted with more recent research which challenges the idea of crowds as irrational.

Discussions of prejudice should allow you to pull together quite a few issues within social psychology, such as conformity, persuasion, ethnocentricity, attitude formation etc. It can also be used as a way of discussing the limitations of psychological research, since knowing why people are prejudiced isn't the same as stopping it. Contrasting different manifestations of social prejudice may be useful here. Another key issue is how we understand language, and how the use of sexist, racist or emotive language influences expectations.

DEVELOPMENTAL PSYCHOLOGY

History & methods of developmental psychology

Developmental psychology raises the question of how and why people change and adapt as they become older. This area of psychology embraces both biological and cultural perspectives in human development, and so enables students to become aware of the way that these, and other levels of experience, interact.

Students should also be encouraged to study human beings within a historical context. Both child rearing patterns and the theories which psychologists have developed about child development change with the economic and political changes in society. Perspectives on gender and roles can also be explored in this context, and serve to emphasise the dynamic and flexible nature of the human species.

This area also provides an opportunity for teachers to explore some philosophical roots of psychology. The Hobbesian view that society is necessary to control our inherently bad nature can be contrasted with Rousseau's notion of the child's inherent innocence. Both can be challenged by Locke's contribution that, mentally, we are born as a blank slate (*tabula rasa*). Contrasting these three perspectives allows the student to discuss the role of upbringing in determining human behaviour. In terms of psychological schools of thought, Watson's behaviourist stance can be contrasted with Gesell's emphasis on genetic maturation, and this in turn can be contrasted with Piaget's notion of an epigenetic landscape, seeing the developing organism as a ball in a landscape of hills and valleys, with life-choices aiding or inhibiting development. This enables the modern dialectical and interactionist perspective to be set within a historical context,

and can also help students to perceive development as a mixture of continuous and discontinuous changes.

The different emphases within developmental psychology can be explored by looking at the research of writers like Piaget, Vygotsky, Freud and Bowlby. These psychologists set the agenda for future developmental theorists, and they pulled on different ideas as sources of inspiration. So, for instance, Piaget drew heavily from biology in his theory of the child's acquisition of knowledge; Bowlby drew heavily from both psychoanalysis and ethology for his theory of attachment and personality development; and Vygotsky's emphasis on social interaction and culture leads to a focus on linguistic and social communication.

Finally, the way that developmental psychology has changed during the past century can be discussed within the framework of advances within research methodology, increased awareness of ethical issues, and the increased acceptance of qualitative methods.

Infancy

There are several key issues to raise when looking at infancy, because the infant's world is very different from the adult's. In the early years of life the child's perceptual, motor and intellectual development change considerably, so one task of developmental psychology is mapping those changes. Students need to be diverted, however, from seeing this mapping as the be-all and end-all of developmental psychology, and to be encouraged to explore underlying mechanisms and principles of development.

One of the major changes in developmental psychology has been the challenge to the idea that the neonate is a prisoner of its own limited senses, living in the "blooming, buzzing confusion" described by William James. This early view tended to result in psychologists perceiving the infant as an "inferior" being, and focusing primarily on the infant's lack of ability. By contrast, recent perspectives argue that the child's world is meaningful from an early stage, and this view has produced a considerable amount of research on infant competencies.

Links between early development and later development can be explored through research on early attachment and how this may predict later styles of relationships. Research on both "enriched" and deprived children can broaden the discussion, as can cross-cultural studies. It is important, though, to avoid the deterministic idea that such outcomes are fixed for life, and you may like to draw on the work of Rogers to show how childhood insecurities may become resolved in adulthood.

More specific research topics, such as visual and linguistic development, can be used to investigate theoretical concepts such as sensitive or critical periods in development. Indeed advances in technology have enabled psychologists to link even foetal development with later development such as left-handedness. The use of research to support or reject these theoretical debates can be discussed, along with the range of methods used to study babies, and how adequately they really do explore these issues.

It is also important to stress the role of adults in aiding the child's development. Some theories which are useful for doing this include Bruner's notion of scaffolding and Vygotsky's ideas about a zone of proximal development for the child's developing intellect.

Early childhood

Language acquisition is one of the major developments in early childhood. For humans, oral history and culture are crucial in aiding the child's entry into the world. The link between the child's language and thought can be examined by looking at the work of Piaget, Bruner and Vygotsky. Studying the work of Vygotsky, in particular, enables links to be made between language, culture, and human interaction. Looking at the history of psychological approaches to language acquisition allows students to compare different theoretical perspectives, particularly through the Skinner/Chomsky debate over language acquisition.

Students might also like to consider whether language is uniquely human, and how the child's acquisition of language influences both their understanding and their perception of their world. This can be useful in enabling links to be made with comparative psychology. Attempts to train chimpanzees and gorillas to use language raise questions of both ethics and the transference of knowledge, as well as allowing students to discuss species specific behaviour.

The study of early childhood allows students to explore social development as well as intellectual development. For instance, the function and changing nature of play can be discussed in the light of Vygotsky's work on the zone of proximal development. The use of cross-cultural studies and research on children born either blind or deaf can help to uncover universals of development and the role of experience. The child's awareness of gender and roles also allows students to compare psychoanalytic, cognitive and behaviourist theories.

Donaldson's critique of Piaget's research stresses the importance of understanding children's behaviour in its social context, as does much recent research into early childhood. Similarly, research on autistic children helps to illuminate what can inhibit social and cognitive development, as well as providing insights into cognitive functioning by demonstrating how children might excel in one area, whilst being apparently "deficient" in others. Donaldson's work also encourages students to evaluate the link between research method and theory.

Middle childhood

Owing to the Piagetian dominance in developmental psychology, much of the study of middle childhood has been concerned with either amplifying or challenging Piaget's ideas. This type of work includes questions about whether Piaget mistook a culturally specific Western form of intellectual adaptation for a biological universal. There are also problems about how children make the transition from one mode of thinking (e.g. pre-operational) to another (e.g. concrete operational); and whether the boundaries between pre-operational and concrete operational thought are really that strict.

Moral development, too, was largely dominated by Piagetian thinking, although Kohlberg, Freud and the behaviourists provided some alternatives. It is worthwhile discussing whether there is a necessary link between moral reasoning and moral behaviour and whether the use of stories is the best method of assessing moral reasoning. More recently, interest in moral development has also focused on the child's developing social awareness, and the child's theory of mind.

The more modern perspectives emphasise the social nature of child development, and one of the best examples of this is the work of Judy Dunn. Dunn's observational research emphasises the importance of naturalistic research, and her studies clearly reveal children's abilities to understand emotions, and to empathise with others at a much earlier age than was previously thought. By studying children in their own homes, she was able to explore the role of siblings in understanding emotional development, and her work stresses the importance of the emotional context of child development.

Children demonstrate abilities outside of the school context which do not reveal themselves within the school environment, so it is important to consider why this should happen. Studies of Brazilian children reveal that they are fast and accurate when working out mathematical problems about selling food in the street. In the classroom, however, they use different methods for arithmetic calculations. This raises some questions about whether schooling actually aids understanding, in real terms. Is it, as Vygotsky suggests, that children switch from perceptual based reasoning to verbally based reasoning once their competence in language increases?

Cross-cultural comparisons also raise other questions about the relationship between cognitive ability, social influence, and the nature of the material to be learned. Do some languages make the children's schooling easier, in that Italian children can spell all the words they can read, whilst British children often have spelling lagging behind reading? Why is it, for instance, that in China arithmetic was traditionally seen as the easy school subject while language and literature were seen as more difficult and advanced, whereas in Britain the reverse is the case?

The problems of assessing children's intellectual abilities at this stage can also be explored by focusing on the controversy that surrounds intelligence testing. Is intelligence inevitably a culture-bound term, and does the assessment of a child's intelligence result in labelling and self-fulfilling prophecies? Is intelligence truly only an adjective, and not a noun? How do modern conceptions of intelligence, such as Sternberg's triarchic theory or Gardner's multiple intelligence model, help us to deal with these questions?

Adolescence

The topic of adolescence leads almost inevitably into discussion of the historical and cultural influences in human development, and may also throw light on the presence or absence of biological universals. Whilst adolescence may last nearly a decade (or longer!) in Western cultures, in other cultures such as the !Kung San of the Kalahari Desert, adolescence is rather less lengthy, with children of that society being self-sufficient by the time they reach puberty.

Cross-cultural research also raises questions about the usefulness of the notion of stages, which may be of value when considering some of the major Western theorists. As ever, Piaget provided a baseline for the psychological understanding of changes in adolescent thinking. This type of approach is partly mirrored by Keating, who distinguished five aspects of adolescent thinking that marked its difference from the concrete operational thought of middle childhood.

Current research also enables students to challenge the idea of a single cognitive developmental system, and to explore the idea of systems which are both content- and context-specific. It is also worth encouraging students to consider other variables that may contribute to changes in the adolescent's thought processes, such as a greater ability to process information due to increased memory through greater use of symbolic representation, and a greater fluency in the use of language.

Students should be encouraged to explore some of the limitations of the various kinds of methodology used in this area. Cross-cultural research inevitably raises questions of ethnocentricity, and students also need to consider very critically the type of problems which Piaget used to demonstrate formal operational thought. Recent research in this area strongly suggests that everyday reasoning may be quite different from the reasoning adopted in formal test situations.

It is also important to consider changes in personal identity during adolescence. One useful vehicle for doing this is contained in Erikson's work. This allows for an exploration of role changes and other important features of the adolescent experience, and may allow us to consider whether single experiences or initiation ceremonies can change an individual's perception of themselves from a child to an adult. It is also worth encouraging students to consider whether contemporary societies also have their own version of initiation rituals and ceremonies.

Modern psychology also frequently challenges the earlier idea that adolescence is inevitably a time of storm and stress. Other perspectives, such as the lifespan approach or Coleman's focal theory, take a different view, which may be more appropriate to the majority of experiences. The importance of peer groups and gender identity also needs to be discussed, and locating this within a historical and cultural framework can often be useful in aiding the student to get an overview.

Development in adulthood

One of the most interesting questions in developmental psychology is the question of why our knowledge of psychological development at the different ages is so unbalanced. There is a vast amount of psychological research into infancy, a great deal on early childhood, somewhat less on later childhood and adolescence, and very little indeed on adulthood and old age. Moreover, most of the latter has only emerged during the past three decades.

One of the few earlier psychologists to attempt an overview was Erikson, whose theory of psycho-social conflict resolution spanned the entire lifespan, although even Erikson identified more conflicts in the first decade of life than at other times. Students may like to consider why this imbalance should exist, and why it may be changing in recent years. It is worth raising questions such as the idea that changes within society, like the insecurity of continued work and a higher rate of divorce, may have led adults to re-examine their identity and their capacity for intimacy. This challenges the assumption that adulthood is a stable, unchanging period or an inevitable decline towards death.

Levinson's stages of adulthood have been criticised as being too normative, and assuming that everyone follows the same basic pattern of life, or ought to. It is also useful to get students to question whether the notion of being "on time" or "late" for such tasks is important. Are people judged socially by taking "too long" to get jobs, get married, and/or produce children? Such stage theories also raise the question of whether, if people don't fulfil these tasks, they are somehow less mature. It is worth encouraging students to identify the implicit value judgements which are often contained in stage theories, as they can often pass unnoticed.

Indeed, the term adulthood itself is worth examining in some detail. There are many ways that adulthood can be defined: biologically in terms of reproductive capacities; socially in terms of roles and economic independence; psychologically in terms of one's personal identity and values; and so on. In this context, Freud's suggestion that the two basic needs of adulthood are love and work can also be explored, along with the idea that adulthood involves a struggle between the desire for security and the desire for freedom.

Research on adult development has tended to fall into two strands: the lifespan approach which focuses on how adults change over the years in terms of their cognitive, physical and social abilities, and the life-course approach which looks at the influence of life-events. These issues can also be explored in terms of gender identity, since much of the early research on adulthood can be criticised for being modelled on male development.

Research methods for both approaches can be problematic, but they also reflect the changing paradigms of psychological research methodology. The "cohort effect" often confounds research on studies on lifespan development, and longitudinal studies are difficult to undertake. Realistic research into life-events of necessity needs to adopt a less experimental research framework, and therefore also provides some useful examples

of qualitative methodology, including the use of retrospective accounts and interviews.

It is also useful to explore whether the phases/stages of recovery that psychologists suggest follow many life-events, such as divorce and death, are prescriptive rather than descriptive, and whether such information does actually contribute to our understanding of the human being.

The topic of old age allows students to explore issues about social prejudice and implicit assumptions, as represented by stereotyping and ageism. It is also valuable to bring in cross-cultural research here, particularly with respect to the idea of old age as a time of wisdom and social respect. Inevitably, the topic raises the question of whether chronological age is less important than one's social roles, economic independence, and physical health. The idea of age as a period of development is another valuable theoretical tool for encouraging students to identify and challenge unthinking social assumptions.

INDIVIDUAL DIFFERENCES

Introduction
Initially, students often welcome a discussion of individual differences, since it holds out a promise of looking at why people are unique, instead of searching for the general laws thought to explain us all. However, the promise often remains unfulfilled, and it is worth exploring with students why this should be so.

One argument is that in its attempt to be scientific, the study of individual differences has invariably resulted in comparing people along a continuum such as intelligence, personality, or normality. Rather than studying uniqueness, therefore, it has come to focus on similarity, looking at how some of us measure up as scoring more or less on a given dimension than others.

"SO WE ALL AGREE GENTLEMEN; THAT EVERYBODY IS UNIQUE."

Key issues to raise within this area include why some of the differences between people are seen as being more important for scientific study than others. For example, psychology has focused more on intelligence and personality than, say, physical competence in sporting activities. This inevitably raises questions about cultural priorities. For example, one issue here would be the socio-cultural background of the rise of the study of intelligence at a time when society was changing from an ascriptive to a meritocratic basis. Another might be the cultural principles of some African peoples of it being an affront to humanity to enumerate, count or measure people. The nature–nurture issue is also at the forefront of discussions of individual differences, together with notions of continuity. Does our personality/intelligence/vulnerability to mental disorder remain the same throughout life? What factors contribute to changing us, and how does this happen?

It can also lead to questions about whether people should be compared along dimensions in the first place, as well as the question of who decides which dimensions to use, and why. Should awareness of the diversity of humanity be encouraged, rather than a classification of human nature into a relatively small range of categories, which inevitably means that much of the richness of human difference is ignored or denied?

Intelligence & intelligence testing

Since intelligence as a concept is very much in the public domain, students are unlikely to approach the psychological study of intelligence without some prior opinions. These can make for lively discussions, as well as interesting essays.

One of the first questions which comes up is what intelligence actually is. Students might explore how psychological views differ from those of lay people, and whether it is actually possible to measure something that is so tricky to define. It is possible to argue, too, that the more recent approaches to intelligence, in particular those put forward by Sternberg and

Gardner, may be closer to lay understanding of intelligence than some of the older theories.

The newer approaches of Sternberg, linking intelligence to cognitive psychology, and Gardner, broadening the range of abilities contributing to intelligence, can raise questions about whether intelligence is a general ability, or a group of special abilities. This also allows you to discuss factor analysis, and the role of hypothetical constructs as explanations for differences. Do we need to use the term "intelligence" to explain why Mary solves maths problems more quickly and with fewer errors than Jim?

The issue quickly leads on to a consideration of reification, and the question of whether intelligence should really be treated as a noun, or whether it is really an adjective for describing an action, observation, or something similar. It is also important to discuss why people want to measure intelligence at all, and the implications of this type of research for people who are deemed to be less intelligent than others.

Inevitably, any introductory treatment of intelligence leads you into the nature–nurture debate. Although modern models, such as that of Sternberg, allow a more integrative approach, so much of the history of intelligence testing has been structured along this dichotomy that it is not possible to avoid it. Equally, it is not possible to avoid the socio-political dimensions of the debate, and this can lead into some interesting discussions about the social responsibility of science and ethical issues in psychological research.

Exploring nature–nurture issues also leads to questions about the nature of scientific evidence, and what specific data actually implies. It can lead on to the whole question of whether tests are reliable and valid along with the difficulties involved in standardising tests. It raises questions of culture-free and culture-fair testing, and issues about norms, standardisation and cultural assumptions. In particular, it is important to discuss ethical issues when exploring differences between ethnic groups.

Can we have a definition of intelligence, let alone a test of intelligence, which is entirely culture free?

Personality: Factor theories

The topic of personality allows you to discuss a range of issues within psychology. By getting down to the nitty gritty of what people are actually like, it provides a picture which spans the whole question of perspectives. It's worth bringing these to the fore.

Firstly, you can explore whether trait or type models of personality adequately explain differences in behaviour. For instance, June going to a party while Fred stays at home can be explained in a variety of ways. To what extent do trait or type concepts of personality provide us with a useful explanation for these differences? Does the trait of "shyness" or the type of "introvert" actually help us to explain and understand particular behaviour, or is it simply a tautology?

There is the question, too, of the difference between type and trait approaches, particularly with the earlier models. Is the distinction between trait and type approaches that useful? Is it realistic to attempt to categorise people in this way, or do we lose so much information in the process as to make it not worthwhile?

Secondly, the topic allows you to explore the dynamic aspects of human growth. To what extent is personality stable? Do we change over time, and if so, what types of events can change us?

This very quickly raises the nature–nurture issue, and the question of whether heredity plays an important role in determining our personality. The extreme alternative, as put forward by Mischel, is to regard the whole concept of personality as intrinsically unhelpful, since human behaviour lacks consistency from one situation to the next. But what are the middle grounds?

Another issue is to what extent does it help us to take an interactionist approach between different perspectives and levels of explanation? If someone is snappy when they arrive at college one morning, how might other levels of explanation interact with trait approaches to explain their behaviour?

As with intelligence, the topic of personality raises questions of assessment and application. How do we assess personality? Are questionnaires really a good way of sampling behaviour? Are we the best judge of our own personality or do other people have a more objective view of us?

The range of tests used can be explored along with the problems inherent in personality testing. If personality tests are being used for occupational selection, why should people tell the truth? Is there any incentive for them to do so? Do lie scales and knowledge about acquiescence factors and social desirability help us to get round these problems?

The subject can also raise discussions of reductionism, as the uniqueness of the human being becomes reduced to a numerical score in a test. To what extent does factor analysis tell us more about the person analysing the factors than about personality? How far do the factors selected, and the questions asked, reflect cultural values? If people don't appear at the extremes of the trait, are they lacking in personality because they are "just average"?

Finally, the topic of personality raises questions of responsibility as well as cultural issues, and these can be highlighted most clearly when we consider criminality. To what extent does the notion of a criminal personality have any mileage in helping us to understand stealing? How far do type and trait theories of criminality reflect an older, reductionist form of psychology, rather than a modern, interactionist approach which can take into account social factors as well as personal dispositions?

Cognitive approaches to personality

By getting to the heart of the matter, which is what people are actually like, this topic highlights the very different models of the human being which underlie psychology. For example, both cognitive and socio-cognitive theories can be contrasted with physiological perspectives, which suggest that our individuality arises from our genetic/biochemical structure, and the behaviourist view that we are the products of our reinforcement histories. Their emphasis on personal interpretation contrasts with the external orientation of type and trait theories, and also with the emphasis on conscious and unconscious awareness of our motives and needs in psychoanalytic theory.

In other words, this topic can enable you to discuss how different psychologists perceive the nature of humanity. Are we, as Kelly suggests, scientists, continually making hypotheses about the world? Are we, as Rogers suggests, basically good, needing genuine empathetic unconditional regard to grow, or is the Hobbesian view of humanity more appropriate?

The topic also raises questions about psychological study, and whether, for instance, the humanist phenomenological stance of theorists like Rogers benefits our understanding of psychology. Can these approaches be considered to be "scientific" or not? Are they amenable to scientific investigation? Or has the psychological concept of "scientific" become a strait-jacket for the discipline?

The approach of the three principal personality theorists emphasises the importance of what goes on inside our heads; how this affects our perception of ourselves and others, and how this in turn affects our behaviour. This raises a number of interesting questions. As with much of cognitive psychology, the discussion of how we know, or can find out, what's going on inside people's heads can be raised.

It also allows you to raise questions as to the adequacy of each of these approaches. Can we really sort out people's personal problems simply by changing how they construe their worlds? And if so, how far does this extend? What about a Somalian refugee, for instance? At some point, there are issues of power and social reality which need to come into play, but at the same time, adjusting personal constructs can often help people. So where do we draw lines?

Then there's the question of whether we know ourselves best. Rogers assumes that, under the right conditions, people will have all the insight that they need. But just how much insight do we actually have into our own motives? Is non-directive counselling really adequate, or do we sometimes need guidance? And are we truly likely to reveal our innermost thoughts to a therapist, even if we do like and trust them, or are there some things that we will always keep private?

There is also the question of imitation and social learning. How far do role models account for our behaviour? This can lead you into some interesting discussions about nature–nurture issues and family influence, such as is personality "shaped" by role learning in the family? Can the family-transmitted manic-depression found in isolated communities such as the Amish be explained in terms of social learning, as children learn ways of responding to stressful situations from their parents? How important, too, are self-efficacy beliefs? Do they, as Bandura implies, determine our willingness to try something new? Or are there other factors involved as well?

The topic also leads into some of the ethical issues involved in changing people's thinking. Who is to decide that our personal constructs need fine-tuning, or that our self-perception doesn't match up with our experience? Are we actually intruding on people's right to self-determination when we deliberately set out to change how they think?

Approaches to abnormality

The whole area of abnormality raises issues of power, social control, and ideology. Who defines people as abnormal, and what happens to them once they are given the label?

This becomes apparent as soon as we begin to look at the problems of defining either abnormality or normality. It is worth raising the question of whether we are looking at a continuum of forms of behaviour, with normality at one end and abnormality at the other, or whether the normal and abnormal are discrete classes. In which case, is it simply that the normal are "us" and the abnormal are "them", or is there a more robust justification?

The question really is whether we can ever pin down abnormality without relating it to its socio-political context. Historical and cultural perspectives clearly raise the issue of ideology and social control when we look at past definitions of "mental distorts" — for example, "drapetomania" (slaves running away from their masters, which was interpreted as a pathological condition). Although students often tend to see these as simply an example of a misguided past, while modern society is free of such "illusions", it is worth raising some modern equivalents. What about "hyper-activity" in children, for example, or the idea of the psychopathic terrorist? Earlier in this century, homosexuality, masturbation and unmarried motherhood were also considered disorders in need of psychiatric treatment. All of these provide insight into shifting social values and opinions about abnormality.

The use of a statistical definition also raises the problem of the minority actually being right in certain cases (everyone in the Middle Ages had lice—did that make it a good thing?). It also allows you to explore why some minorities are given a higher status than others (e.g. people with high IQs).

This topic also allows you to explore the pros and cons of using taxonomies to classify people, as well as raising the inevitable problem of reliability and validity of diagnoses. Rosenhan's study raises issues of ethics, both in social and medical practice and in psychological research. The study involved deceit, but the results were of undoubted social utility. Where do we draw the line?

It also raises the question of social labelling and self-fulfilling beliefs. How far do we believe that people truly recover from "mental illness", and how far is an episode of this kind a social stigma which stays with that person for life? Why do people react so strongly to the idea that someone might be mentally ill?

Finally, the three main models of mental illness can be explored in terms of how they portray its cause. This also raises questions about the perception of the mentally ill, but this time as contained in the theoretical model. Are such people to be seen as individuals with high hopes of being cured once we know enough about biochemistry? Are they to be seen as people with behavioural disorders who can be changed by changing reinforcement schedules? Or are they voyagers into "inner space", perhaps haunted by their past and present circumstances, and trying to make sense of the world? Couldn't it be argued that the real world is an OK place to visit, but not a nice place to live in?

The issues of free will and determinism can be examined by looking at how much responsibility the models give to the mentally ill. It is also important, though, to stress that within each of the schools of thought there are quite heated debates between the adherents, and that more eclectic approaches are beginning to be used.

Forms of pathology

The vast range of behaviour which shelters under the umbrella of psychopathology immediately raises questions about the diagnosis and causation of disorders. How easy is it to classify people as schizophrenic, depressed or having a personality disorder? How different is that process from diagnosing that someone has glandular fever, cancer or AIDS?

The range of potential causes allows students to link causation with the earlier models of mental illness. It also opens up the idea that some disorders might be more readily explained by the medical model, while others are more suited to psychoanalytic or behavioural explanations.

The use of twin studies as a means of unravelling the nature–nurture issue can also be explored, in their social contexts as well as in terms of the evidence available. For example, Kallman's work on twin studies in schizophrenia led to anyone with that diagnosis being automatically sent to Nazi extermination camps. Less dramatically, there is the question of recovery which accompanies the diagnosis: we can have a physical illness and recover from it, but how far are people really considered to have recovered from an episode of schizophrenia? What does the diagnosis "schizophrenia in remission" really mean? And how does it affect the person's future life?

This raises questions about the somewhat tautological use of diagnosis. These can be explored by looking at different descriptions of diagnostic categories and behaviours. For example, activity "characterised by hostile, negative and deviant behaviour" is labelled as "an oppositional deviant disorder". Does the label merely describe the behaviour? In what sense does it constitute an explanation? This also brings us back to the many of the issues about traits and social explanation which arose in the discussion regarding factor theories of personality.

It is important to raise cultural as well as individual issues when discussing deviant behaviour, since what may be perceived as deviant in one community isn't so perceived in others. This leads you into questions about the professional's desire to change the behaviour of "deviants". Laing and his followers argued that, in many cases, the deviant is probably more sane than the so-called "normals". Is the real problem actually about creating a more tolerant society?

Therapeutic approaches

When looking at this area, it is important to stress that the diagnosis of mental illness isn't always easy. Any discussion of therapeutic approaches also raises the issue of how we know whether someone is no longer suffering from a mental disorder, and who determines whether this is the case. What factors should be taken into account when determining the effectiveness of any treatment? The relatively limited research into the effectiveness of therapy raises its own questions.

Different psychiatric treatments can be linked to the four different models: somatic therapy, including drugs, surgery and ECT, focuses on changing the structure and biochemistry of the individual; psychotherapy stresses the importance of understanding earlier experiences in the hope that understanding can lead to change; behaviour therapy emphasises the need to change behaviour using techniques based on both classical and operant conditioning; and cognitive therapy stresses the need to change ways of thinking. Students may raise the question of other forms of therapy, such as family therapy, and these can be related back to theoretical approaches in previous topics.

Discussing the different types of treatment allows you to encourage the students to explore the nature of applied psychology. Is it about understanding human behaviour and experience, or is it about changing it? The moral and ethical dimensions of this come to the fore in discussions of somatic therapies such as ECT and in behavioural methods such as aversion therapy. Ultimately, both of these

are all about suppressing disturbing symptoms. But how far do they contribute to our understanding of human experience, or to positive future action?

There are also significant ethical questions which arise with respect to the type of psychiatric treatments available for various disorders. Most notably you might discuss the side effects of some types of somatic treatments (lobotomies, ECT, drug therapies etc.). This raises questions about the nature of the assumptions underlying the treatments themselves as well as about the lack of follow-up research into their effectiveness. Is it really true that psychiatric therapies only change when another treatment comes along to replace them?

Discussions about conditioning allow you to explore the relevance of animal research as indeed do studies on learned helplessness. To what extent can we generalise from research on animals to humans? Does the fact that humans have language and reflective mental abilities invalidate some of the claims of the early behaviourists? Few modern psychologists would accept the idea that people are nothing but stimulus–response ping-pong balls. Is it therefore still appropriate to use language and methods of treatment which are based on that assumption?

Particular problems are raised by the use of irreversible treatments like leucotomy or lobotomy to control problems like "anti-social personality", especially when these terms are applied to criminal behaviour. There is also, in the case of more innocuous treatments, the question of the use of control groups who are not given any treatment which could actually benefit them. Yet, if we don't use control groups, how do we know whether therapy is effective or not?

You might also invite students to consider whether this whole issue is entirely irrelevant, since all psychiatric treatment is ultimately "faith-healing", and the different theories simply provide people with explanatory frameworks which suit them, and so allow for the faith-healing to take place. Do these widely differing theories persist simply because having more than one available model means that most people can find something to believe in? Would any of these methods work with someone who was deeply sceptical about its basic assumptions?

BIOPSYCHOLOGY

What is biopsychology?

For many students of psychology, biopsychology is a new approach to understanding their own and others' behaviour. For this reason, it can be profitably compared to other approaches within psychology, particularly social psychology, cognitive psychology, and comparative psychology. Such a comparison can help the student to understand the concept of levels of explanation.

Comparing physiological psychology with other areas of the discipline can also help students' understanding of reductionism and determinism. By showing how human beings can be studied from more than one point of view, the idea that any one point of view provides the only "real" explanation is easily challenged. In physiological psychology, reductionism takes the form that understanding the functions of the nervous system will eventually tell us everything there is to know about people, but the insights which we can obtain from other areas of the discipline show that other levels of enquiry also have something to offer.

When discussing reductionism and its alternatives, there are two important concepts. The first is that of *emergent properties*: the observation that human activity is more than simply the sum of its physiological elements, and that entirely new aspects of behaviour or experience can emerge when complex systems are combined. The second is that of *interactionism*: getting away from the idea that

behaviour has just one single "cause"—whether physiological or not—but is produced by many different aspects of experience interacting.

The complexity of both our internal and external environments needs to be emphasised, along with the idea that knowing how individual parts of a system work doesn't necessarily explain how the system works as a whole. Given the subject matter of biopsychology, research methodologies are often ingenious, and students might be encouraged to look at these in terms of the tricky problem of teasing out the various factors, as well as in terms of the ethical issues involved.

The question of animal research is also one which needs to be raised at an early stage, since so much of our knowledge of physiological mechanisms derives from animal experimentation. Students need to be aware of the basis on which physiological research generalises from animals to humans, and in particular the concept of evolution, which underpins our whole approach to the area. In addition, the ethical aspects of animal studies are likely to attract student attention, and the way that criteria regarding animal experimentation have changed in the light of these concerns is very relevant here.

In the end, of course, students will make up their own minds on the question of animal research. But the study of biopsychology also allows the teacher to explore whether the means justifies the end, especially when looking at research undertaken on Alzheimer's disease, AIDS, and cancer.

The nervous system

One obvious starting point for discussing the nervous system is to focus on its function as a communications network, passing information to and from central and peripheral receptors around the body. This raises the question of how we manage to do this, given the fact that the nerve impulse is, at least theoretically, electrically identical on each occasion. It allows the student to distinguish between types of communication, such as the electrical transmission of neural impulses and the chemical transmissions which operate across the synapse. It also allows students to explore issues of coding: the use of inhibitory and excitory synapses, neural pathways, information conveyed by the number of neurones firing, the volley principle, and so on.

Discussion of the nervous system can also encourage the student to consider the variety of ways that we can study how that system works. This includes comparisons with other species, research on chemical and electrical transmission, scanning and electrical monitoring, as well as the use of physical destruction and interesting case studies.

Studying the organisation of the nervous system connects its structure with its function. Most teachers will find it useful to focus on the somatic nervous system, the autonomic nervous system, and the brain. However, it is important to stress that the division of the brain is a matter of arbitrary classification, and that other divisions are equally possible.

Evolutionary considerations can be useful in giving students a framework, and so avoiding an unstructured list of parts and functions. The idea that the reptilian brain stem and cerebellum may to be responsible for reflex actions, the paleo-mammalian limbic system and primitive cortex may be responsible for emotional responses, and the higher mammalian neocortex may be responsible for higher cognitive processes does provide some structure, and may help students to get a grasp on the complexity of the brain. It is useful for students to see the brain as a synthesis of past evolutionary trends and interaction with present experience. However, it is also important for them to recognise that this is, essentially, an oversimplification.

It is also important to point out to students that whilst we have found out a great deal about certain parts of the brain, such as the sensory and motor cortex and the visual system, what we don't know far outweighs what we do know, and there are very large parts of the brain whose function remains essentially unknown. This is particularly true of the association cortex, and the way that this is involved with higher cognitive abilities, personality and consciousness, but it is also true of many other parts of the brain, such as those mediating emotional experience.

Language, hemisphere function & memory

One of the important things to bring out when teaching this topic is where the evidence has come from. The extensive use of case studies raises questions about why those individuals were being subjected to clinical scrutiny in the first place, and so leads into the observation that they were, unavoidably, different from the norm. It is also important to emphasise the interactive nature of brain functioning, in that damage to one area may produce a problem because that area represents a link in a chain or an element in a system, rather than because that area directly produces the function concerned.

The idea that different types of language function are mediated by different parts of the brain raises a number of questions about modularity, interactions between different areas, the complexity of interaction between neural development and environmental experience such as in the case of the angular gyrus, which demonstrates how brain nuclei may develop in response to particular types of experience, and the question of social labelling, for instance in the case of dyslexia. Students can be encouraged to explore all of these issues while learning about this topic.

Many students find the idea that the two halves of the brain may mediate different types of experience fascinating, and one of the most important messages is to convince them that these are simply general tendencies, not absolute distinctions. It is worthwhile emphasising the difference between the

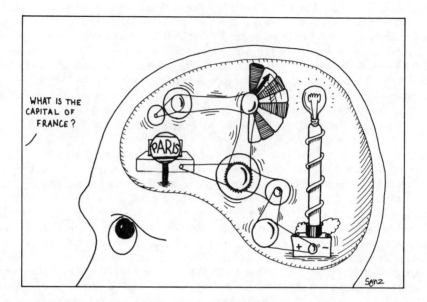

scientific conclusions which can be drawn from this research and the semi-mystical exaggerations which have resulted from inaccurate popularisation of it.

Hemisphere differences also raise interesting questions about research methodology, and the point at which research techniques become so specialised that they may cease to resemble how the brain processes information in everyday life. Concern about the atypical nature of initial research participants in this field may have resulted in innovative experimental research on people without brain damage, but perhaps the stimuli needed to reach these conclusions are too specific.

Hemisphere function also allows the teacher to explore left handedness and other aspects of brain function, although it is crucial to stress that there is no such thing as the "standard" brain and that general trends for a population may tell us very little about any one particular individual. Students also need to be introduced to concepts such as within-group and between-group variance when looking at topics like gender differences. It is also

important to stress the role of practice and training in influencing brain function.

Putting together the evidence for learning and memory in the brain is a complex task, and students may be helped if they are encouraged to distinguish between structural evidence—different parts of the brain which may be involved—and neural evidence, such as the influence of neurotransmitters, long-term potentiation, and the like. Making cortical and sub-cortical distinctions when considering brain structures may also be helpful.

This area also inevitably raises questions about different types of memory storage, and whether remembering where food can be found is the same as remembering how to get into bed, or the names of brain structures for an examination. Once these types of questions have been raised, it becomes obvious that both animal research and case studies are the key elements in aiding our understanding of learning and memory. The variety of amnesias allows students to explore whether problems in memory may be due to storage problems, as is the case with temporal lobe amnesias, or whether they may be due to deficits in retrieval, as seems to be the case with sufferers from Korsakoff's psychosis.

Stress, anxiety & emotion

Given the world we inhabit, it is essential to understand some of the reasons why we experience stress and anxiety, and the relationship between physiological states and external stressors. While it has proven difficult to define stress and anxiety in psychological terms, it is clear that certain physiological systems have a key role to play in our understanding, notably the pituitary gland and the ANS, as well as the role of hormones.

The study of mechanisms involved with emotion raises a number of questions about the mind–body relationship, and the role of cognitive appraisal in human experience. Students might also be encouraged to reflect on the balance of psychological research in this area: why is it that psychophysiological research has focused so extensively on the negative emotions of fear, anger and anxiety, and not positive ones as well? While it is true that we have not identified physiological mechanisms involved in happiness or contentment, it is equally true to say that very few people have bothered to look for them. That leads into questions about bias in research funding as well as social assumptions about what types of experience count as important.

It is worthwhile explaining Selye's work on the General Adaptation Syndrome, and examining whether the types of factors leading to stress have changed over the centuries. There is also the question of whether different types of stress lead to different types of reactions and actions. It is useful to distinguish between short-term reactions to threatening or anxiety-provoking events and our physiological responses to long-term stress, since these can be very different in terms of their effects on the individual.

Research on stress and anxiety also emphasises the role of individual differences such as personality types A and B and gender differences, though it is crucial to examine the limitations of this type of research, particularly with respect to the latter. It is worth bringing out the distinction between retrospective and prospective studies of personality differences in stress response, since this highlights ways of getting round some of the problems presented by retrospective methods.

The question of animal research and its ethics also comes to the fore in this topic, and these can also be linked with questions about the validity of the methods used. For example, Brady's research on executive monkeys was not only ethically dubious but also confounded by his picking the most active monkeys to take part in the research.

It is also worthwhile exploring the variety of ways that people cope with stress, including drugs, psychotherapy and cognitive therapy. This investigation can emphasise the relationship between the cause of anxiety and stress and the mode of treatment. It can also give the student some insight into the idea of the paradigm, and the way that different types of explanation and intervention are accepted by different groupings within the scientific or professional community.

Sleep, arousal & motivation

The Yerkes–Dodson Law of arousal is one of the more useful concepts of everyday psychology, in that it is able to clarify a number of aspects of everyday experience. Psychology students, however, need to recognise that there is not just one simplistic type of arousal, but that the term is often used to describe several different mechanisms, ranging from the orienting response of attention, to the extreme state induced by feelings of rage.

The role of the reticular formation in mediating states of arousal of the body, and evolutionary questions about how this system evolved and why it might have been an advantage to organisms which possessed it, can help students to identify core aspects of the

SECURE IN THE KNOWLEDGE THAT HIS BODY'S RESERVES WERE
RIGIDLY MAINTAINED, TREVOR AWAITS PHYSICAL ACTIVITY....

concept. It also provides a framework to distinguish between different types of arousal.

Biological rhythms also raise questions about different aspects of everyday experience, including the role of both internal and external factors in the control of these rhythms. The most apparent of the different types of biological rhythm is the circadian rhythm, and this becomes most apparent when we consider phenomena such as jet lag and shift work. However, there are also many other types of biological rhythm, both infradian and ultradian, although our knowledge of the physiology underlying many of these processes is relatively limited.

Discussion of the function of sleep enables the student to explore different perspectives: the ecological approach which focuses on life-style and position on the evolutionary scale; the physiological approach which stresses sleep's role in repair and makes the interesting distinction between REM sleep repairing the brain and slow wave sleep repairing the body; and the neurological approach examining the role of noradrenaline and serotonin, which has contributed to our understanding and use of drugs to aid sleep. The way that these perspectives each give us different insights into the sleep process again shows the value of levels of explanation as opposed to reductionism.

Studies of sleep deprivation raise ethical issues, both in terms of the use of non-volunteer human research participants (as in the army studies) and in terms of animal studies, such as those which show that rats die after 21 days of total sleep deprivation. This topic also raises interesting questions about military influences on the values underpinning research funding, e.g. why has sleep deprivation been extensively studied, while the type of restricted sleep experienced by new parents has not?

One of the most important caveats to bear in mind when studying the physiological basis of motivation is its very limited range. We know very little about whether there is any physiological influence in more complex human social motives, since research in this area has focused entirely on basic physiological motives, or at least motives which are easy to measure in animals. Maslow's hierarchy of needs and McClelland's work on achievement motivation are outside most of the physiological research on motivation, and raise questions about the uniqueness or otherwise of the human being.

The use of needs, drives and motives to explain behaviour raises questions about the role of explanation within psychology, since the existence of a drive is often invoked to explain behaviour, while the behaviour is assumed to be the evidence that the drive exists, resulting in circularity. This can lead on to questions about what constitutes scientific explanation, and how far scientific activity involves description rather than explanation.

Research into both hunger and thirst raises issues about peripheral versus central mechanisms in the control of intake. It also points quite clearly to the role of the hypothalamus, and the importance of homoeostasis in regulating our internal environment. Concepts such as the set-weight and studies of obesity in rats do raise some parallels in human beings. But closer scrutiny shows that simplistic parallels are inevitably inadequate, and that other levels of explanation also need to be evoked to explain human obesity or anorexia.

The existence of non-homoeostatic motivation (exploration, play etc.) shows that even in animals physiological levels of explanation do not provide a full answer. Research into electrical stimulation of the brain raises interesting questions, too, about the distinction between purely physiological reward and reward mediated by environmental factors. It is important for students to be aware that the study of this area actually shows us how little we know about motivation, rather than how much.

Sensory information processing

When teaching about the different types of sensory reception, one of the key concepts to get across is that of *transduction*. No matter what form the information has when it first arrives, chemical, physical pressure, light etc., it is all converted into the one form which the brain can use: neural impulses passed along neurochemical and neural pathways. Students can therefore be encouraged to consider the range of ways in which the sensory receptors transduce the incoming information, and this will provide a key to understanding why the receptors for the different senses take such very different forms.

Pain perception raises a number of questions about the relationship between mind and body. The gate theory of pain shows explicitly how higher-order processes such as cognition and motivation can influence sensory perception, and the various neural pathways in the simplified gate theory model reflect that complex relationship. Topics such as phantom pain also raise questions about the brain's internal representations of the body, and how it is functioning.

The sense of smell also raises interesting questions, particularly about the role which smell plays for human beings. The fact that smell pathways don't synapse in the thalamus but instead make a direct connection with emotional and motivational systems suggests that techniques such as aromatherapy may be tapping into some very ancient biological systems. Even though we are often unaware of it, smell can sometimes unconsciously manipulate us, through moods and reminders, and possibly even pheromones. The possibility of manipulation through pheromones also raises questions about subliminal perception, as well as the role of cognitive as opposed to biological input in human sexuality.

It is worth reflecting on the way that hearing and vision, the two most important senses for human beings, also seem to have the simplest number of basic elements, in both cases representing wavelength (pitch, colour) and amplitude (loudness, brightness). Attempts to map the basic elements for the other senses come out with far more dimensions such as elements of taste. If we consider the complexity of visual experience (art, reading etc.), and of auditory experience (music, vocal intonation etc.), and also the way that we train children in visual and auditory perception but not in the others, we may end up asking about the quality of information which might be provided by the other sensory systems, with their greater number of dimensions.

There are other interesting parallels, too, between auditory and visual processing, and in particular, the way that the incoming information is analysed at quite an early stage to identify its basic properties and is then followed by later analysis which performs a re-synthesis of the information. The process also suggests ways that top-down information, or organising principles such as Gestalt forms, can influence the later stages of the analysis. But the existence of blind-sight reminds us that simple, linear models of visual information processing are not enough—there is still a great deal that we don't know.

COMPARATIVE PSYCHOLOGY

Comparative psychology & evolution

Perhaps the first question which needs to be raised in looking at comparative psychology is just what are we comparing, and why?

Comparing behaviour between different species can be just as enlightening as comparing animal behaviour with human beings, and comparative psychology is concerned with both. In each type of comparison, both similarities and differences can give us important information.

It is also important to try to distinguish between comparative psychology and social biology, since so much of the basic knowledge overlaps, and research in each discipline feeds into the other. Effectively, the difference is one of emphasis: comparative psychology is concerned with what we can learn from the process of comparison—what it tells us about underlying general mechanisms of animal behaviour and/or cognition—whereas for the most part (although there are, of course exceptions) social biologists are concerned with mapping out social processes within one species.

One useful framework for this is provided by Tinbergen's description of the four areas of research in comparative psychology: development, mechanisms, function, and evolution. Although social biologists are interested in these areas as well, they represent the prime focus for comparative psychology, over and above biological description, and analysis is applied as a means to that end.

Comparative psychology also allows the behaviour of human beings to be explored within a broader biological, ecological and socio-political framework than many other areas of psychology. The subject raises key issues about the nature of the human species, and encourages debates on biological determinism and reductionism. Are we, as some socio-biologists suggest, "gene carrying mechanisms" whose main aim is to reproduce genes? Are we "underdeveloped apes", as neoteny maintains, or are we to be distinguished from the rest of the world because we have language and culture? Or does some combination of these apply?

It is also essential to stress the wide diversity of animal behaviour, since what works exceptionally well for one species could lead to the annihilation of another. Along with the diversity of behaviour one finds a diversity of theories and explanations of the behaviour, and these can be examined to give students a historical perspective of the subject. For example, you could consider the rise and fall of the concept of "instinct" as a means of explanation. Descartes' notion that "humans act, animals react" can be traced throughout recent Western thinking, and may be a useful concept for students to either apply or react to, depending on how they interpret the evidence.

It is also important to examine the key concepts in this area, such as the various forms of evolutionary theory, so that the complexity of the subject is highlighted. The notion that human beings are somehow at the top of some evolutionary tree, and the concept of the phylogenetic scale, raises interesting questions about anthropocentricity; as well as the question of human rights and responsibilities towards other living creatures who share the planet.

And, of course, it is always interesting for students to consider the selective use of animal research in supporting various ideological stances, especially in discussions of gender roles and aggression.

The basis of behaviour

Any examination of the basis of behaviour raises the question of genetic and environmental determinants of what the organism actually does. Perhaps one of the most important principles of this field of study is the fact that the issue is not about "either/or", or the relative amount of influence. Instead, both genetic and environmental influences interact to produce the end result.

However, the process by which this conclusion has been reached has involved a number of theories which attempted to separate the two, and to present either one or the other as the source of animal behaviour.

Students need to be encouraged to move away from the simplistic nature/nurture dualism, into a more interactive perspective. Discussions of the distinction between genotype and phenotype, along with well-known studies like Hailman's "How an instinct is learned" and the research into biological preparedness can highlight some of the principles involved.

The discussion of the basis of behaviour also allows students to explore the role of models within psychology and whether they aid our understanding or merely oversimplify issues, as is suggested by the hydraulic model of aggression. They can also be explored in terms of their generating research to support or reject the model.

It may be a useful exercise to look at what type of evidence would be needed to convince scientists that a form of animal behaviour really was governed by one or other factor. Indeed, it is in this historical context that much of the experimental work on inherited and learned mechanisms in the behaviour of specific animals needs to be interpreted. Students can evaluate the methodology used to explore this issue, along with the ethical considerations of such research and the relevance or otherwise of the problem being addressed.

One of the central issues when looking at explanations of learning is how far the apparently mechanistic or associative forms of learning are actually influenced by cognitive processes such as expectation and anticipation. These can be examined by focusing on the difference between traditional and more recent models of both classical and operant conditioning, along with a discussion of other types of learning such as latent learning and insight.

The survival value of certain types of behaviour can be examined by looking at behaviour which appears to result from a clear-cut interaction between genetic preparedness and environmental stimulation.

This includes one-trial learning such as the rejection of food and drink after sickness, and behaviour which has been acquired during critical and sensitive periods. Students should be encouraged to interpret this behaviour—indeed, to interpret all of the evidence—within an evolutionary context.

Courtship, mating & reproduction

One of the most important messages to get across when teaching this area is the difference between analogy and homology. Animal studies of courtship, parenting and attachment have attracted a great many facile analogies, but even a cursory glance at a range of species reveals a rich diversity among species in these areas. This means that many of the common assumptions made by "pop" ethologists about what is "natural" in human behaviour become somewhat dubious.

That doesn't mean, though, that students need to become swamped in a morass of biodiversity. When trying to teach them this subject, it is useful to direct students' attention to the environmental demands on a given species, and to encourage them to consider the evolutionary pressures which have given rise to these particular practices. It is no coincidence, for instance, that a particularly rapid form of attachment such as imprinting evolved among species whose young were physically capable of getting around independently very early in life. By looking at environmental function and evolutionary adaptation, and by drawing in concepts such as the ecological niche, students can be encouraged to see that the many different forms of animal behaviour were not invented solely to upset people taking exams, but do make some sense in their own contexts.

This area of comparative psychology also allows students to expose the many myths that abound in society about the roles of males and females. The idea that females always, or inevitably, look after the young of the species is challenged by ethological research, and the idea that the strongest male always gets the female is challenged by studies of the male red deer, where a younger male may mate while the dominant male is fighting off a rival. The area also raises discussions about the role of co-operation in gaining a mate, clearly showing that competition is not the only mode of behaviour in animal life. It is worthwhile considering why studies of males rearing young are less likely to be cited in support of child-rearing patterns in human societies than others.

It is also useful to draw attention to some of the challenges to the "selfish gene" theory presented by the tendency of non-related members of some species to rear the young. The link between the mechanisms which have evolved for rearing the young, and the type of offspring produced, in terms of whether they are altricial or precocial, aids understanding of the link between behaviour and developmental and environmental factors.

Finally, the whole topic can be explored in terms of different degrees of flexibility offered by having a more or less highly evolved capacity to learn. Primate behaviour as a general rule tends to be more flexible, and more susceptible to individual difference and prior learning, than the behaviour of birds. This carries an evolutionary message in its own right, as well as highlighting again some of the dangers of confusing analogy with homology.

Social organisation

Research into the social organisation of different species introduces the student not only to the diversity of forms of social organisation, but also to the diversity of explanations offered to explain why such social structures evolved and how they are maintained.

The key topic areas are aggression, territoriality, anti-predator behaviour, social structures and reconciliation. It is worth noting

RODNEY HAD HIS OWN IDEAS ABOUT 'NATURAL' WEAPONRY.

that this is a somewhat wider range than the traditional trio of aggression, territoriality and dominance. This reflects more recent areas of interest on the part of researchers, and students might be encouraged to reflect on how, and why, the focus of interest in comparative research has changed over the century.

The explanations offered range from specific explanations which focus on survival of the genes, or more broadly-based ones, which link particular styles of behaviour to ecological and other environmental factors which can and do change. Students might also be encouraged to evaluate mathematical modelling as an approach, in terms of questions such as what constitutes explanation, the usefulness of idealised approximations, and so on.

It is important to emphasise notions such as adaptation to ecological demands and change, to avoid students falling into the trap of seeing human nature—or even the nature of higher

primates—as somehow fixed. It is also important to stress that similar forms of social organisation don't necessarily result in the same behaviour, since despite sharing a similar social organisation the stumptail monkey is far less aggressive than the rhesus monkey.

Indeed, explanations of aggression allow students to explore wider perspectives within psychology. It is interesting to note, for example, which particular research projects have been used to "explain" some of the excesses of humanity. So despite studies revealing that strict territoriality is rare among primates and seasonal territoriality or range is the norm, and studies which show that linear dominance hierarchies are actually quite rare, both phenomena have been used to "explain" human wars. It is discussions of these topics that highlight the dangers involved in making simplistic generalisations from one species to another, and from animals to humans.

This area of study can also be used to highlight the way that the metaphors we use to describe social structures can end up distorting our perceptions of what we are looking at. The use of terms like "sedentary" rather than "resident", or of the term "harem" to describe the relationship between a group of hinds and a stag can illustrate the power of metaphor to shape our thinking, and, more importantly, to reveal deep-rooted, but not necessarily accurate, assumptions about likely forms of animal social organisation.

Communication & information

Any study of animal communication raises questions about the purposes and functions of communication. The different definitions show how easy it is to get embroiled in complex issues such as intentionality, and deception. So it is important to emphasise to students that sensory reception provides a *potential* channel for communication, not an inevitable one: any given sensory mode may or may not be used as a way of communicating by the animals concerned

The range of different modes of communication is enormous and enables links to be made with environmental constraints, social organisation and specific issues such as the risk of being attacked by predators.

The rich diversity of signals also raises the question of whether human beings are at the top of some evolutionary tree, in terms of communicative ability, or whether in fact our awareness of the world around us is rather more limited. After all, we don't hear infra- or ultrasound, have no electrical detectors, are insensitive to polarised light, and so on. Students might consider the idea that, as in other species, human communication has simply taken the form which best enabled us to deal with our environment, or environments.

The study of birdsong provides a neat example of Tinbergen's four areas of comparative psychology: ontogeny, mechanisms, function and phylogeny. Each of these has been studied, and revealed new insights. These four areas may also be used to structure what we know of communication in other species, such as bees or chimpanzees.

Studying communication also implies drawing inferences about what a signal actually means. This issue comes to the fore when looking at the communication systems of whales and dolphins, where interpretation is difficult owing to our limited knowledge, and their very different lives. This also raises questions about the validity of our inferences about other forms of animal behaviour.

Perhaps one of the most interesting areas revealed by the study of animal communication, and particularly birdsong, is the links which it makes between inherited mechanisms and learned experiences. Different bird species reveal different degrees to which their songs have been inherited, and the concept of the sensitive period provides a link between behaviour which is entirely inherited and that which is entirely learned. These evolutionary links can be taken further by the studies of animal "words" and natural categories.

Finally, the research investigating critical and sensitive periods often involves isolating young animals, or some form of permanent or temporary deprivation. This can be evaluated in terms of ethical considerations, as well as methodological issues.

Animal cognition

The notion that human beings are somehow distinct from animals because they think and have free will can be challenged by studies of animal cognition. Studies of imitation, curiosity, concept formation and cognitive maps clearly reveal that something is going on inside the animal's head, although the difficulty is in establishing just what it is.

You can use this difficulty to focus students on issues about research methodology, comparing the ethological approach with its emphasis on natural observation, with the experimental approach of the behaviourists. You may also find it interesting to compare research on animals with research on babies since both cannot tell us what they are thinking. This can easily lead into discussions about justifiable assumptions, and possibly back again to the question of the uniqueness of the human being.

The range of different forms of animal cognition which has been studied invites comparisons, such as which of them really do provide convincing evidence about animal cognitive abilities, and which are less so. Is pigeon homing of the same order as exploration, self-awareness, or language, for example?

The numerous studies which involved training animals to use a variety of forms of human communication and symbolic codes raise this question in yet another form. While Terrace's arguments undoubtedly torpedoed these research programmes, there are many who feel that his assessment was biased in an unwarranted manner, and extremely unfair. At the same time, it would be unreasonable to assume that all of the attempts were equally successful. Students should be encouraged to appraise the various studies and methods systematically.

The research also raises ethical concerns, especially in regard to what happens to the animal once the research funding is terminated, or the animal becomes too big to manage. There are ethical questions, too, about keeping dolphins and whales—species accustomed to roaming large areas of sea—in captivity, whether for benign research purposes or not.

Research on animal cognition enables links to be made between the physiology of a species and its cognitive ability. The comparative studies of the evolution of the cerebral cortex raise interesting points about its role in the development of both human and animal intellect.

One of the most interesting issues to be raised is the notion of the interaction between genetic and learned mechanisms in adapting the individual to its environment. Research into prepared learning implies an evolutionary continuum between things that an animal is very ready to learn, things it can learn fairly easily, things it can learn but only with some effort, and things which it will not learn at all. This idea of adapted learning calls into question the whole idea that genetics and learning might somehow be opposing mechanisms, and may also help us to understand how the human being evolved as it did.

3

Class or seminar activities

INTRODUCTION

In our experience, students learn best when they are able to relate what they are studying to everyday life, or to things that they themselves have done. Experienced lecturers and teachers accumulate a wealth of examples and activities which help this to take place; but the novice lecturer or teacher often has much less to draw on. This chapter allows us to share some of our own classroom experience, as well as some of the many tips we have received from other lecturers in our time. We hope that this will be directly useful to those who come new to teaching introductory psychology, as well as, perhaps, giving some fresh ideas to experienced lecturers or teachers of psychology.

This chapter is all about ideas for getting your students actively involved in their learning. It contains many different suggestions which range from simple interpersonal activities to formal classroom debates. The suggestions cover all of the different areas of introductory psychology, and each theme is divided into categories, which means that for almost every topic you should be able to find several suggestions. As a general rule, most of the suggestions are suitable for groups of between 6 and 30 students, although you may find some which can be adapted for the larger scale lecture.

Not every group of students, of course, will take to every kind of idea. Some students love acting out social roles or other parts; others prefer to stay in the background. Some students thrive on formal structured exercises, others find them restrictive. Most students benefit from group work, though some are extremely intolerant of group activities which don't seem to lead to an obvious goal. For this reason, most of the group activities which we have suggested have a very clear structure, and/or an obvious task to complete. Whatever students you have, though, we feel that the range of activities and ideas provided here will mean that you can always find something to help to liven up the subject matter just that little bit more.

PERSPECTIVES ON PSYCHOLOGY

Introduction

One way into asking students to think about what psychology involves is to ask them to think about how people respond when they say that they are studying psychology, and whether the response would be different if they said that they were studying English or maths.

Alternatively get the students to collect different definitions of psychology over the last 100 years (or you could provide them) and analyse how the definition has shifted from the "study of mental processes" to "the scientific study of behaviour".

To introduce students to a historical perspective you might ask them what types of questions people would have asked about human beings over 2000 years ago. If the students are keen, you might try to discuss what school they think Aristotle or Plato or Kant might have adhered to. The role of technology in theorising could raise issues about computer analogies replacing archaic ideas such as Plato's wax tablet for explaining memory.

To challenge the notion that psychology is simply common sense, divide the class into groups, and get them to discuss the truth or falsity of a series of proverbs which are obvious contradictions (e.g. "absence makes the heart grow fonder" as opposed to "out of sight, out of mind"). The disagreements and tendency for students to say that "it all depends" allows you to distinguish between personal experience and scientific research.

Descartes' search for the soul can be discussed by asking the students where they think their soul resides. The mind–body link can also be explored by discussions on meditation and the use of biofeedback. If your students are interested in philosophy you might want to get them to contemplate the implication of brain transplants.

Finally, you could raise some of the problems of introspection by asking students to say what is going on inside their heads in three different situations: e.g. when talking to a friend, when riding a bike, and when contemplating last night's experiences. They could also consider how much control they have over their thinking.

Current approaches & historical roots

A good starting point for looking at the different approaches in psychology is to provide the students with a blank chart with the following headings, which they have to fill in: Approach, Key Psychologists, Main Areas of Interest, Methods of Study, Key Theories, or Concepts, Applications, and Evaluation.

Try drawing it up on a large sheet of paper for use as a wall chart, and get different groups of students to decide what should be entered for the different areas. Alternatively, different people or groups could take different approaches and present their findings to the rest. Drawing up such a chart can also lead you into other discussions, such as why so few major psychologists mentioned in the textbooks are female.

Another possibility when you are introducing students to the study of approaches is to take one example of behaviour, such as forgetting someone's name, and to look at how the different schools of psychology might explain it. For instance, psychoanalysts might explain forgetting in terms of repression; cognitive and developmental psychologists might discuss it in terms of information processing; social psychologists might interpret it in terms of significant and non-significant others; and biopsychologists might focus on damage to the brain.

Set different groups of students to focus on specific areas of psychology while discussing the same problem, and then get them to feed back their ideas in a general session.

It is fairly easy to explore some of the strengths and weaknesses of the different approaches by trying out aspects of their methodology in class. For example, free-association can be explored by giving the students key words like "mother", "life", "school" and asking them to write down the first words that come to mind on hearing them. Inevitably, students come up with similar responses which allow you to discuss the role of culture, rather than repressed memories, in generating responses.

You might also go on from here to discuss the role of culture in explaining Freud's initial interpretations of his findings, most notably his original conclusion that the memories which his female clients had of early sexual abuse from their fathers are factual memories, rather than his later conclusion that they were unconscious wish fulfilment.

Behaviourism can be explored by asking students to list the reinforcements that they have experienced during that day, and the situations in which they received them. You might also get them to decide on suitable reinforcements for encouraging appropriate behaviour, and to discuss what aspects of their own behaviour they would want to control.

Abnormal psychology can provide a fund of ideas for looking at the free will vs. determinism debate. The area also allows you to explore the role of responsibility. Should one impose behaviour modification techniques on drug addicts? Should schizophrenics be forcibly given drugs? To what extent does "mental illness" exonerate someone from taking responsibility for their actions? Get the students to collect examples of mental illness used as explanation in newspaper reports, and use these as the basis for discussions of society's use of the concept.

It is also worthwhile considering whether changing how people think can change their behaviour, and vice versa. Try setting up a formal classroom debate between those who believe that it can, and those who believe that it can't.

The relationship between cognition and behaviour can be examined when looking at cognitive therapy. Try collecting examples of irrational thoughts, and looking at how they might be changed. Beliefs about exams are a good area: begin by asking each student to list five common beliefs about exams, and then to indicate which ones they personally agree with. These can be used as the basis for a class discussion—and also allow you to slip in some ideas about actually using some of the implications of memory and other psychological research!

Finally, you might ask students to collect examples of behaviour that they think challenges the socio-biologists' view of the selfish gene, such as adoptive parents, helping elderly people in the street, and so on.

Major issues in psychology

A good starting point for major issues in psychology is to ask your students to shake hands with the person next to them. Then ask them to explain why they did it. This allows you to introduce levels of explanation, ranging from socio-cultural explanations (obeying the teacher or lecturer, or the cultural significance of the handshake) to physiological levels of explanation (how the brain interprets sound waves, neural impulses stimulating muscle contraction to produce movement).

Try asking your students to write down why they chose their particular subjects of study. You can then move on to the question of how much choice they actually had, and thence to questions about free will and determinism. Alternatively, ask them to analyse how different kinds of psychological determinism (social, behaviourist, etc.) might explain their choice.

The complexity of the nature–nurture debate can be introduced by getting the students to collect examples that correspond with Lerner's different levels of environment: from the inner biological level (i.e. physiological influences on the unborn child) to the socio-cultural level such as the influence of social identification. Alternatively, bring physiological conditions such as phenyl-ketonuria (PKU) to your students' attention, since this is a good example of how a condition produced by genetic factors can be alleviated by a change in diet (i.e. environment).

Keep an eye out for media coverage regarding genetic influences, and ask students to bring in any cuttings from newspapers which refer to genes. Do a content analysis on them. Keep a particular look-out for articles which suggest that a gene has been found to explain either criminal behaviour or homosexuality. These are helpful for exploring

"...THAT'S BETTER...FIRST DAY ON THE JOB, SON...GOTTA LOOK SMART..."

how an extremely complex issue becomes oversimplified in the press, and for looking again at questions of reductionism vs. levels of analysis.

The role of environmental factors in development can also be explored by looking at the American ideas of "hot-housing". Are we trying to advance human capabilities or pushing too hard? Does society truly want intelligent people anyway, or are they just as likely to become social misfits? Try setting up a classroom debate on one of these questions.

The area of consciousness raises the classic philosophical questions of "how do we know we are not dreaming?", and "how can we find out what someone else is thinking?". If your students are philosophically inclined they might enjoy debating these issues.

Alternatively, get classroom groups to research different aspects of consciousness,

such as dreaming, hypnosis, drug effects, sensory deprivation, artistic creativity, blind-sight etc., and to report on what they have discovered. This should lead you into discussions about the relationship between self-awareness and consciousness, and other issues such as whether people can have memories of events that never really happened.

Motivation & emotion
Both motives and emotions are frequently used in everyday speech to explain our own and other's behaviour, so a good starting point is to encourage students to consider the usefulness of these concepts. Try asking them to list five emotions and to discuss the role they play in explaining behaviour.

You might also extend this exercise to explore the differences between human emotions as experienced in everyday life, and human emotions as portrayed through the media. First, ask your students to write down five emotions (including positive ones) which they have experienced during the past couple of days. Then ask them to note down the emotions which they see portrayed in one episode of a TV drama or soap opera. (You can do the same thing for motives, but it is best to keep the two separate). How closely do the two match up? And which view of emotional experience is most closely reflected by psychological research?

Try asking students to list ten examples of the "pushes" and "pulls" in life—drives (like hunger) or goals (like passing my psychology exam). Get them to consider why increasing extrinsic motivation, such as paying amateur sportspeople, often decreases intrinsic motivation.

Present students with McDougall's list of drives, and ask them to criticise it. For example, what is meant by a submissive drive?

The notion that different people set different kinds of goals can easily be discussed by asking the students to list some short-term, mid-term and long-term goals. Don't be too surprised if they don't come up with all that many!

This is also a good place to introduce the modern concept of *manageable goals*, and the positive benefits these can have on self-efficacy and self-esteem. For example, you could set the students into groups, and ask each group to suggest three manageable goals which would ultimately help them to pass their psychology exam.

If your college is trying to introduce appraisal, you could get the students to think of some objectives which could be included in mission statements.

Emotions can be introduced by getting the students to classify emotional responses in terms of the five main components—the cognitive, physiological, experiential, expressive and behavioural components. Alternatively, you might get them to compare two different emotions such as love and anger along these dimensions.

You might even want to persuade the students to take part in a Laird-like study by getting them to smile throughout your lesson to see if it really does influence their emotions towards you.

The important role of cognition in interpreting emotions can be explained by asking students to discuss the difference between seeing someone die in a Hollywood movie, and seeing someone shot in real-life being shown on the news.

Research methods

Research methods are probably one of the easiest areas to teach in the classroom, if you remember to give the students lots of concrete examples. Throughout the course, get students to evaluate research work, perhaps by using a check list that includes ecological validity, ethics, experimenter bias, sample, etc.

You could try taking a very simple idea like asking how they would find out if they actually learn better in the morning or the afternoon. Alternatively, ask them to devise studies to challenge the somewhat naive comments which people often make about people, e.g. "blonds have more fun", "redheads have bad tempers", etc.

The difference between "evidence" and "proof" can be explored using the "classic" activity in which students are set into groups and told to regard themselves as a research team with a large, but not unlimited, research grant. Their task is to find out once and for all whether violence on television leads to violence in children. This introduces them immediately to the idea of operational definitions, and since different groups tend to devise different types of studies, it also allows you to introduce the idea of *triangulation*: no one study will be definitive, but if enough different types of evidence point in the same direction, we may become reasonably certain of our conclusions.

The problem of establishing causal relationships can be explored by looking at correlations and getting students to consider all the variables that might explain the links such as between watching violent TV and being aggressive.

The links between theory and empirical data can be explored by asking students how they respond when their own research disproves well-known theories. Alternatively, invite them to consider the scientific status of psychology by getting them to give examples of psychological studies that predict, control or aid understanding. Ask your students to look at journals of psychology and analyse how many of the reported studies support existing theories and how many challenge them.

The difficulties involved in observation can be demonstrated by asking students simply to "observe someone", preferably during their break. The problems of deciding what to observe, when to observe and how to observe become immediately obvious. This can also allow you to distinguish between subjective and objective research, in that deciding whether someone is happy is very different from, say, timing how long it takes someone to eat a piece of toast.

Get the students to draw up a large chart, listing topics in psychology down the side, and with columns for research method used, examples, etc. Do some areas of psychology make more use of case studies, or other methods, than others?

The conduct of research

One of the easiest ways into this topic is to present the students with the British Psychological Society's ethical guidelines, and ask them to look back through their notes and collect examples of research that breaks the code. If this is near the start of the course you might give them some help by suggesting that they research Zimbardo, Milgram, and Asch. Having looked at the examples, you might ask the students to consider whether there are alternative ways in which the information could be gained, and if so, what these are.

It is also worthwhile linking the conduct of research to social psychological mechanisms which can help to explain why participants are reluctant to withdraw from a study once they agree to take part. You could also try giving examples of cases where they might feel obliged to break the code, e.g. if a participant in a study on mood revealed that they were contemplating suicide. This could be useful in introducing students to the need for judgement in ethical decision making.

You can also give students examples of research and ask them to classify which particular psychologists could potentially be sued by research participants, e.g. for the Zimbardo prisoner–guard study, for the Sommer research on seating in libraries, and so on.

As you teach the course, invite students to keep a chart of ethical concerns and specific studies which raise them.

Reports of research in the media often have ethical implications, whether or not these are actually raised in the report. Invite students to collect such accounts, and to bring them into class. This might include medical and biological research and accounts of specific cases, as well as specifically psychological studies.

Case studies can also be looked at from an ethical point of view, as there are controversies over the publication of research from the patients' point of view, as well as some potential for in-fighting over who is the key researcher. This is particularly pertinent to the case study of Genie.

Students are often concerned about animal research, so you could try and get them to find three animal studies that they think really did contribute to our understanding of human behaviour. If they feel the task is impossible, get them to find cases that they consider have contributed nothing other than showing human cruelty.

A classroom debate on animal research is always sparky, and can be very useful in helping students to clarify their views on the matter.

Give students examples of contentious findings and discuss whether they would publish those papers or not. Classic examples could include the research undertaken on twins in concentration camps in Nazi Germany, or research suggesting that some humans are better than others (notable in the area of race and intelligence). Use these concerns to raise awareness of the role of science in contemporary society.

Try setting your students into groups to develop a set of principles which will establish the limits which should be placed on the search for knowledge; since unlike the physicist or chemist, the psychologist is studying its own species. This should lead into discussions of whether the end justifies the means, and what we actually sacrifice if we ignore ethical concerns.

COGNITIVE PSYCHOLOGY

Sensory systems & perception

When you're teaching this topic, it may seem as though it simply consists of a number of different bits of information which don't really relate all that well to one another. If you're trying to get students to see it as a more coherent whole, one possibility is to use the topic of perceptual organisation to pull the topic together. Since learning, experience and physiological hardware all contribute to what we see, it may help your students to realise how the parts can contribute to the whole. For example, a topic like figure/ground organisation can be used to co-ordinate why particular aspects of neural organisation in the visual cortex and thalamus are like they are; pattern perception in infants; Gestalt principles of perception; and computational theories of perception. Other topics in perceptual organisation, such as depth perception, provide similar scope for co-ordination.

For many students, the study of sensory systems can be their first taste of physiological psychology, and in some cases, they can become overly concerned about the need for an extensive knowledge of physiological detail. It is important to stress that they are not being trained to be physiologists or biologists: that a detailed understanding of neural mechanisms is not essential. It is important that they get a *general* picture of what is happening, and become aware of the limitations which neural hardware places on our ability to interpret the world.

In real terms, this means that students need to get some kind of grasp of what sensory systems are doing as they transmit information to parts of the cortex, and of how the brain can pass information from one area to another. They also need to acquire some appreciation of the principle of transduction, at least in so far as they understand that what the brain has to make sense of is a set of electrical impulses, rather than a little picture. They also need to realise that sense receptors take in the information for which they are suited. The absence of sense receptors for some kinds of signals (like, say radio waves) means that we don't perceive them, but this doesn't mean that they don't exist.

One of the easiest ways to get students to begin to think about perception and sensation is to pick up a book and ask them what they see. Steer the resulting discussion towards (a) the idea of sensation: a patch of colour; is the visual image really rectangular, etc., (b) perception as interpretation: how do they know it's a book; does it say book on it? and so on.

You can stimulate a good discussion about perceptual development research methodology by asking "how do we find out what babies can see, since we can't ask them?".

An alternative is to begin the topic by dividing your students into small groups and asking them to devise a study to find out what babies can see. Comparing the ideas produced by the different groups can bring out some interesting methodological (and sometimes ethical) issues.

Use OHPs to show a series of contextual pictures and then an ambiguous image like a series of numbers and then the B/13 figure; or a series of birds followed by the rabbit/duck figure.

Introduce pattern recognition by showing them all of the different ways of writing the same letter, e.g. A,s in different scripts and types.

Get students to produce illustrations of each of the Gestalt principles of perception by using different combinations of As and Bs.

Using an item in a slightly incongruous context, such as having a shoe on a table in your final session and asking students to explain how they perceive it, can sometimes be used to pull different ideas together.

A good example of illusory movement occurs when sitting in car-washes or stationary trains.

Attention

It is possible that when teaching this topic, you could find that students initially find attention a pretty straightforward topic, but then get bogged down by the "models, more models and even more models" approach to the subject. However, this can be to your advantage if you use it to (a) draw out questions about the role of experimental research in theory building, (b) discuss the issues raised by building up understanding of a topic in a piecemeal fashion, and (c) encourage them to contrast this with other models of attention which see it as positively choosing to include things, rather than as filtering them out, such as Neisser's schema model of perception.

Another good way of approaching this problem might be to encourage students to approach it from a detective's point of view, e.g. Broadbent's ideas seemed OK until new data blew it for him: the filter leaked...

It's worth encouraging students to think about how these things affect their own lives. They often tend to memorise the "cocktail party" examples, despite their dated nature (how many cocktail parties did you attend last year?), but there are lots of other, similar examples around which they will have encountered personally, such as the student canteen. Try setting them in small groups and getting each group to think of three real-world examples each of selective attention and vigilance. Seeing what they come up with will also allow you to be sure that the students really have understood the topics.

As a general opener to the topic, you could ask students to count the number of times you use a certain word or phrase in the next five minutes. Then read them a fairly interesting/lurid piece of prose, and see how many of the targeted words or phrases they notice. (Have the answer ready beforehand.)

If you don't have access to, or time to produce, dichotic listening devices, you can explain the idea by asking one student to shadow what you are saying while the other students attempt to get their attention.

Changing your voice tone while in mid-stream invariably gets the students' attention, and can be used to discuss how and why attentional shifts occur.

Ask the students to keep a diary of any absent-minded behaviour that they indulge in over the week. Then collate the different examples, and discuss whether there are consistent themes and common errors, corresponding to Reason's categories.

Problems of capacity and overload can be introduced by asking students to do simultaneous tasks with each hand, e.g. tapping the head while rubbing the stomach, or rotating one index finger clockwise and the other anti-clockwise.

It's fairly easy to pull examples from everyday life about attention. Try asking them "do you ever do anything else while you're watching TV?" and see what that produces.

Listening in class while writing letters to friends is also another example.

You can draw on your own or other's examples of absent-minded behaviour to explore why people make the errors that they do, e.g. going out with their slippers on, throwing away the potato whilst looking at the peel, forgetting why you went upstairs. This can also be related to major accidents, like aircraft disasters, and then on to the need for good instrument panel design which can prevent disastrous mistakes from being made.

Discussions of initial experiences in learning how to drive a car allow students to explore the role of practice and expertise in discussions of "overload" of capacity. What may have once seemed impossible becomes almost second nature.

Memory
Students generally enjoy the numerous practical exercises which can be used to illustrate different aspects of memory research, but can sometimes find the discussion of theoretical models a bit difficult. It is helpful to make a distinction between the research on "boxes in the head" theories about structures and organisation, and the research on processing.

Some teachers like to use the triple framework of acquisition, storage and retrieval to pull the ideas encapsulated in the areas of sensory systems and perception and memory together. These areas of study include the short-term/long-term memory model; levels of processing, and memory organisation.

The topic of memory is particularly good for enabling us to explore the pros and cons of laboratory research versus everyday experience. The practical implications of the STM/LTM distinction and of the levels of processing approach can be compared. This encourages students to think about which approach relates more readily to, say, their memories for social information (to do with their immediate circle of friends), as well as more formalised types of memory. Theories of forgetting can be used to highlight different reasons why people might forget things in an exam; and a thorough discussion of this could even be channelled to result in ideas about good ways to revise, to make sure that forgetting doesn't happen.

Discussion of how memory is stored and whether we can get early memories back can easily result in sidetracking to discussions of reincarnation, the role of hypnosis in retrieving apparently "lost" memories, and/or why childhood memories disappear. This sidetracking can often be quite useful, especially in allowing you to emphasise important points like the role of expectation and personal motivation in adjusting memories.

Students often find the idea that memory isn't a tape recording very hard to grasp. After all, it feels accurate, and they are sure that it is. One example which often helps to get this point across is to ask them if they've ever been back to see a film which they remembered from when they were younger? And was it different from how they remembered it? Since they recognise that the film is unlikely to have been altered, students can identify that the differences must have come from their own recollections. Taking social examples (like comparing two people's memories of a conversation) is another possibility, although sometimes it can be less successful since there is no objective record to refer to.

When you're teaching about levels of processing, one very useful exercise is to set the students into small groups, and ask each group to apply levels of processing theory to revision. Each group has to develop three different things to do with material that they have to learn for exams. These things have to be based on the idea of processing the material by changing it into a different form. Students often come up with some excellent ideas, and sometimes even put them into practice at exam time as well!

Ask the students to devise a mnemonic for the various explanations of forgetting.

Flashbulb experiences (the Challenger disaster, Thatcher's resignation etc.) often provide an additional interest to discussions about why we recall some events clearly while others seem to disappear.

Semantic organisation can be discussed through discussing initial letter games, like I-Spy, or the TV show "Blockbusters".

Remembering appointments, deadline dates, to do homework, taking medicines, etc. are all useful everyday examples of remembering to do things.

Language comprehension & production

An issue which will come up in this topic is the way that experts often find it very hard to verbalise what is involved in the skill that they are using. This is illustrated quite graphically with reading: asking students to describe what they themselves are doing when they read can provide you with a considerable number of points around which to structure the formal research evidence. Asking them to describe how they normally make eye-movements when reading, and then asking them to observe each other as they read can provide a graphic illustration of the difference between what they think they are doing and what they are really doing. You can also refer to this example later.

A problem which can come up when you are teaching about language is that it's a bit like driving: once you find yourself thinking about it a great deal, doing it becomes extremely difficult. As you talk about language, it can sometimes become quite difficult to work out what you're actually doing when you're using it, particularly if you let yourself get side tracked into philosophical issues. Try to avoid this if you can. Emphasising the way that theories of language have shifted their focus from structural mechanisms to social goals and plans may be a good alternative.

Another problem which can come up when you are looking at theories about the relationship between language and thought is that students often don't like the fact that they haven't got a clear answer about which one is "right". One possible way of using this is to turn it into a team debate, particularly if your students are divided as to which they think is probably more appropriate. Collecting evidence for each side should encourage them to look carefully through the studies about language, and hopefully process them more thoroughly!

Try asking students to count the number of pauses in your speech over a five minute period, as a quick observational study. Then get them to classify the pauses into different types, e.g. pauses at the end of a sentence, pauses to check comprehension, pauses for emphasis, etc.

When looking at language production, try asking students to generate a sentence they've never said before in their life, e.g. "Mickey Mouse decided he couldn't stand travelling by tube, so he took the bus". Then ask them how they did it.

Students often have a very good intuitive grasp of elaborated and restricted codes, which comes out particularly well in role-play exercises.

Give the students sentences like "they are eating apples" to discuss ambiguity. Alternatively, try putting the Bransford and Johnson passage on an OHP and getting them to write down as much of it as they can recall, or to write down what it is about.

Alternatively, language codes might be discussed in terms of familiarity with other people: the use of restricted codes with friends but elaborated codes with strangers or those who are less well known.

The use of inferences in understanding language might also be discussed by looking at the nature of excuses, e.g. "Sorry I'm late, I had a dental appointment".

Processing the written word can be introduced by giving the students nonsense sentences with unexpected bits in: "garden path sentences" like "the black cat the grass" or "the new cars are transporting is expensive", and asking them to read them aloud. See if they find them easier or harder to read than conventional sentences.

Thinking

It is relatively easy for a teacher to get into this topic by giving students a range of problems to solve. Students often love puzzles, and will be quite happy to try them out in class. It's important, though, to make sure that you don't end up making your students feel inadequate or inferior, since many of them will find difficulties when they are trying to solve problems in class. Problem-solving exercises should be fun!

Once you've done a few exercises with your students, the next stage is to get them to think about what is involved. Discussing how past experiences helped them to get the results that they did allows you to lead into questions of mental set and the like. Alternatively, you can get them to analyse the components in a puzzle, identifying initial states, goal states, and if you have the right kind of puzzle, even algorithms.

When teaching decision making, a lot of students can get bogged down with the various heuristics. The best way of getting them over this is to make sure that you always have a good stock of real-world examples of each one to hand. At least at first, don't rely on being able to think of one on the spur of the moment! It doesn't matter if the examples are trivial: applying heuristics to decisions about buying breakfast cereal or deciding whether you should have spent your money on new clothes helps to make it clear and real to students.

Try scanning the textbooks for classic examples of problem-solving exercises to get students to begin to think about what is involved in problem solving. You might begin with Duncker's radiation problem, Wason's selection task, or Luchins' jug example.

Introduce decision making by getting students to think about the number of everyday decisions which they make, like what to eat for breakfast, how to get to college, and so on.

Similarly, get them to run through a typical day, mentally, to identify the range and types of thinking which they actually do (e.g. planning what to wear, concentrating in class, not concentrating in class, day-dreaming, deciding what to do at lunchtime, etc.).

Get your students thinking about concept formation by setting them into groups and asking each group to identify Rosch's three levels of concept with respect to different sets of concepts. (Each group has to think of the three themselves, but if you like you might structure it by asking for an animate one, a domestic one, etc.) Once they've got them, you could always get into a "twenty questions" type of game as the others try to guess what the concepts are. This could lead into interesting discussions about concept-formation strategies.

Judgements and probability could be discussed in terms of risks and diseases: most of your students will have opinions about smoking and lung cancer, ozone thinning and the risk of skin cancer, AIDS and the use of condoms, etc. This can also be contrasted with other conventional risks, such as driving on motorways.

SOCIAL PSYCHOLOGY

Conversation & communication

Non-verbal communication abounds with material for classroom exercises. One of the simplest (but always popular) is to introduce it by showing a series of stick figures one at a time on the OHP, and asking the students to call out what the figure is communicating. If you are feeling rather more dramatic, try going through a range of postures and gestures, and ask the students what they think you are trying to communicate.

Alternatively, you can ask your students how they would communicate the following types of information non-verbally:
- the person that you are shouting your mouth off about has just walked into the room.
- "Please don't continue telling me about your operation, it is making me feel sick".
- "I think you are wonderful", etc.

Try writing them on slips of paper and asking "teams" to act out each one.

Get students to list what types of behaviour they would look for in a nervous teacher. (Not recommended if you're in your first year of teaching, this one.)

The power of eye-contact can be easily demonstrated by getting students to look into each others' eyes and timing how long it is before one person looks away. Proximity can be demonstrated by getting someone to walk as close as they can to someone else and stop when they feel uncomfortable. Do it within the class—though remember that there are ethical issues raised by causing discomfort to others! (That in itself can provide material for some good discussion/debate.)

Strategies in conversation can be discussed in terms of how many times your particular offering gets picked up in group chats. Alternatively, students might prefer to observe someone else and see whether their ideas are taken up or not.

Students might enjoy listing the types of phrases people use to let others know that they have more power or knowledge (e.g. "I was really surprised when I passed 12 GCSEs a year early"). You could, if you like, relate this to rhetorical frames in discourse analysis.

Explore the idea of social scripts by asking students to write down what they consider to be the difference between a script for visiting the dentist and a script for visiting a doctor.

The metaphors of everyday conversation or media analysis also make valuable material for discourse analysis: is the economy/political situation/Royal Family described as if it were a sick person, as a game, or using military metaphors? It is also interesting to discuss what sort of phrases make students wince (e.g. "I'd like to share this with you...", or, worse: "I hear what you are saying, but...").

Attribution theory might be introduced by getting students to explain certain events to themselves and each other, such as a disastrous first date, why they failed their driving test, etc. If this seems a bit threatening, looking at different explanations for why some people are rich and others are poor, or explanations for homelessness can also provide material to compare internal and external attributions.

If a big news story about a court case breaks while you are teaching this area, use it to discuss attribution theory. Why did the person do whatever it was that they did? Was it their fault?

Interacting with others

One way into this topic is to ask students to list three different social encounters that they have had during the week, and then to look at the factors that contributed to their interaction in each one. They might consider areas such as styles of speech, dress, etc. Alternatively, ask them to act out how they change their behaviour when they are with different people, e.g. with parents, friends, partners, colleagues at work, or figures of authority.

Discussing embarrassing events can make an entertaining lesson as well as raising the question of why doing something you perceive as embarrassing in front of other people makes it worse. Be careful of your sensitive students, though: this is definitely a volunteer-only activity!

It is important to remember that while most teachers are familiar with Milgram's research, it is often a real eye-opener to students. Try leading into the topic by describing the situation and asking them how many people they think would obey. Alternatively, begin by asking them to do something a bit out of the ordinary such as changing their seating or moving the back row people to the front, and

then ask them why they did what you told them to do. If you have Milgram's book on obedience to authority, it is worthwhile reading aloud the soldiers' account of the Mi Lai massacre, to bring home the real-life implications of obedience.

If you're feeling brave, you could risk asking your students what they think contributes to someone being a good teacher, to raise issues of leadership. Alternatively, introduce the topic by changing your usual style, e.g. from democratic to authoritarian.

You could combine group research and leadership studies by dividing the students into groups and setting them a task. The classic ones are building towers out of newspaper or bridges out of Lego. Ask the group to describe how they interacted, or alternatively set half the class to watch, as observers.

Another possibility is to get each group to decide on the three most important qualities a leader should possess. You might want them to relate these to real-life situations. Try giving each group a different type of situation, on a slip of paper, and then comparing whether all groups chose the same qualities, then relate this to leadership theories.

If the students are willing, you could divide the class into two equal-sized groups so that they can be paired into observer and observed, and observe the group's activity using a Bales Interaction Process Analysis. This type of analysis allows you to distinguish between task and social leaders, as well as raising the problems involved in observational research.

Alternatively, ask the students to list the categories of behaviour they think would be useful when observing behaviour in groups, and devise a sampling chart from that. The students could then list some of the pros and cons of working in groups.

If all else fails, ask your students to read through their textbooks and come up with several examples of their own behaviour which relates to certain topics, e.g. conformity: standing in queues, laughing at jokes you don't understand because everyone else is laughing, etc.

Person perception, attraction & relationships

A good opening gambit for the whole area of person perception is to begin by asking your students what they notice about people the first time that they meet them.

Alternatively, you could bring in some photos of people who are unknown to the students and get them into groups to discuss what they think about the person. The groups can then feed back into a general discussion to see if there are any similarities in their perception.

Try asking the students to say what height they consider a tall person to be. Students who are under 5'2" will often see 5'10" as tall, whereas those over 6' define 6'7" as tall. You could even try correlating personal height with judgements, if you really wanted. But in any case, this exercise allows you to raise the issue of how far our perception of other people is affected by our perception of ourselves.

It's often quite useful to get students to describe someone that they know well. This allows you to look at the sorts of phrases and words which people use when they are describing others.

Discussions of stereotypes need to be handled with care if you want to avoid reinforcing them. Initially, you might ask students to describe the stereotypical image of a French woman or man, compare them with their stereotypes of Italians, etc., and then ask what relevance this has to their perception of people that they encounter in "real life".

You can also explore stereotypes by getting students to collect newspaper cuttings which they consider support stereotypes, and to explain how they did so.

Self-efficacy can be explored by giving students a range of tasks and asking them how well they think they would do at each of them. You might also get others to judge them on the same dimensions, and see how much congruence there is between the two ratings.

To emphasise some of the problems in researching attractiveness, try asking students to discuss their ideal partner, possibly using film or TV stars to provide exemplars of various personal qualities. However, this does mean that you can end up listening to long debates about the relative merits of Brad Pitt, Daniel Day Lewis and Mel Gibson...

Another way of looking at relationships might be to show the students a brief clip from "Blind Date", and discuss what kind of factors are being taken into account when people are looking for partners.

It is also possible to explore different types of relationships by asking students to list and then discuss the differences between their relationships with friends and their relationships with partners. Be careful, though: while students usually enjoy discussing relationships, it can be a sensitive area. Some people may be having difficulties in their own relationships or their parents may be going through a divorce. Some are not in relationships, and find this distressing. Discussions as to why relationships break up also need to be handled with care.

Finally, social exchange theories of relationships can be explored by getting students to write down the rewards and costs of being in a relationship. Remember to encourage them to look at wider social rewards or costs as well as the personal ones, such as the advantages and disadvantages of being part of a couple in various social situations.

Attitudes

There are several ways of opening up this topic in the classroom. You can start by asking students about the issues they feel strongly about, e.g. abortion (although care needs to be taken to avoid getting yourself into a heated discussion...). Alternatively you might pick a topic yourself, such as charity, and ask the students to discuss their attitudes towards it. For example, does charity help people, or does it let governments shirk their responsibilities. If you want, you could set up a formal debate, with each side having time to prepare its case, two or three spokespeople each, and a vote at the end.

Another way into this topic might be to ask students whether their attitudes towards any issue has changed over the years. Students might mention religious attitudes or attitudes towards homosexuality. Alternatively, you could contrast some of the very old TV shows and some more recent ones, to identify changes in attitudes: sexism and racism, for example, often take different forms in current shows than they did in the 1960s. There are usually enough re-runs of 60s shows on TV to provide material for this.

Problems with measuring attitudes can be introduced by asking the students to write down how they would find out about someone's attitudes towards something like "green issues", or recreational drug use.

Another possibility is to get some examples of questions which have been used in attitude measurement scales, and ask the students to scrutinise them and identify some of the problems involved.

Consistency between attitudes and behaviour provides you with a perfect opportunity to ask students for examples of people acting in ways which contradict the attitudes they claim to hold. Students can usually come up with quite a few of these.

You could introduce the topic of persuasion by asking them whether they have ever watched an advert and been persuaded to buy something as a result. Follow this up by asking them what their favourite chocolate bar or snack food is, and why. The resulting discussions often end up invoking advertising phrases: keep an ear out for them.

Persuasion is a wonderful topic for the classroom, since all of your students will be experts in the field of advertising. Get them to relate psychological concepts to TV adverts which they know, such as analysing advertisements in terms of whether they are appealing to cognitive or affective domains, whether they are giving both sides of an argument, and so on. Students can usually find a current advert for almost every point raised by the classic experiments.

You could also get students to devise an advertisement themselves, using some information which you have given them. Introduce them to the idea of a storyboard for a TV advert, set them into small groups, and ask each group to produce an eight-frame storyboard for their own TV advert. Compare the results. (Incidentally, this exercise can provide good display material for an open day or similar occasion.) It can also bring out a number of questions: what reliable expert would students choose to persuade people to use condoms to prevent the spread of AIDS? How would you persuade the general public to take environmental questions seriously?

If you are teaching this area during a general election or some other major political event it is also worthwhile taking a close look at political broadcasts, and the attitudes which are manifest in them. Get students to identify distinctive phrases, "buzz-words" and metaphors in common use. You can also relate this back to discourse analysis if you have covered that area.

Conflict & co-operation

One way into the topic of conflict and aggression is to ask the students about their fantasies. What would they like to do, or what would they like to happen to someone who has annoyed them or upset them? This often allows you to distinguish between different types of aggression, in that some students prefer physical retribution while others go for psychological ways of getting their own back.

An alternative is to get everyone, privately, to write down a single word or phrase which is the opposite of the word "aggressive". Go round the class collecting all the answers, and you'll usually find that there are several alternatives, each of which implies a slightly different meaning to the original word. This also gives you a good opportunity to raise the question of reification: it's one thing to describe an action as "aggressive", but does that really mean that there is some "thing" called "aggression"? Or is it just a style of interacting?

A good way of getting students to understand different theoretical approaches to the study of aggression is to divide the class into groups and present each group with the same news story, either from a newspaper or by showing them a clip from the TV. Each group would then be asked to explain the news story from a different theoretical perspective: one group taking on a social learning perspective, another a Lorenzian point of view, and so on.

Alternatively, you could organise a formal team debate on the question: ask two sides (choose students with strong-ish views on the matter) to prepare a case for aggression being either inherited or learned. You could limit them to drawing only on psychological evidence, but allow them to range across the syllabus as much as they like. Allow each side two or three speakers in turn, let the team leader do a brief summing up, and organise a vote at the end.

The question of ritualisation in aggression might be raised by looking at sporting activities, such as wrestling or boxing. This can lead you quickly into the debate about catharsis. It may have been suggested by Plato, but does it work?

You need to be careful when dealing with prejudice. The unwary teacher can be taken off guard by both racist and sexist views, and needs to be prepared to deal with them. One way into the topic might be to ask students to imagine that they have absolute power, and can change three things which they think would lead to a reduction of prejudice. What would they choose to do?

It often useful to ask students, singly or in groups, to draw up a list of the advantages and disadvantages of being prejudiced. For example, it has the advantage that it turns you into a cognitive miser in that you don't have to think, but it can also close you off to new information.

Depending on current world events, it is often possible to refer to the way in which certain groups are being represented in the media (e.g. the portrayal of Argentinians during the Falklands War) as illustrations of prejudice. Again, though, this can sometimes lead you into heated debates.

Try getting students to do a newspaper search, and along the way to compare the number of reports of pro-social and anti-social behaviour. Then ask them to explain why there is such a difference between the two. You could follow this up by asking them to keep a list of pro-social and anti-social events which they personally experience in the course of a single day, and compare that with information in the newspapers. Do we usually ignore pro-social behaviour and only remember the unpleasant things? Are the papers deliberately manipulating us into thinking people are evil and nasty, etc.?

Discussion of kin selection might also involve collecting reports about murders, and seeing how many take place within families.

It is worthwhile collecting examples of altruistic behaviour to look at why people help others. This is good for opening up discussions of altruistic behaviour: e.g. stories of people risking their lives to save others help you to explore the notion of self-sacrifice and whether people only do things if they get something out of it.

Students often want to do studies on bystander intervention. One possibility is to arrange for someone to drop their pencil case several times, in corridors or at bus stops, and to note what happens. But there are some ethical questions which need to be raised here, in terms of whether it is acceptable to deceive or manipulate members of the public. Some argue that these studies are ethically unacceptable, so it's worth bearing this in mind.

DEVELOPMENTAL PSYCHOLOGY

Infancy

Get the class to draw up a chart of what babies can do at different ages. Set your students into three groups, and allocate social, cognitive and physical development to each group. They have to discover the information to go on the chart.

You might like to include a "research method" column on the chart, so that the methods used to study babies at different ages can also be compared.

Ask your students to collect articles on "hot-housing" or child prodigies, to explore the role of early environmental factors in development. Classic examples include musicians, chess players, and mathematicians. Use these studies to discuss "enrichment".

In order to get Piagetian stages across quickly, set your students into groups, give each group a list of the stages, and ask each group to give an example from each stage and describe how the stages differ from each other.

Extend this exercise by asking them to collect experimental evidence which (a) supports and (b) challenges the Piagetian stages.

Set up a formal class debate, with one side arguing in favour of Piagetian approaches to development, and the others arguing against. Score points for each valid argument made by each side, and adjudicate to make sure that only *psychological* evidence is considered valid. (The fact that Piaget was Swiss, for instance, cannot be taken as a damning criticism of the theory.)

Ask students to collect case studies of children who have been born deaf, blind or are thalidomide victims. Use these case studies to raise questions about "normal" development. This also allows you to discuss the ethical aspects of case studies, and their contribution to theoretical debates.

When studying foetal development, get students to report on the images of pregnancy and pre-natal development portrayed in the media. Discussions could include the implications of alcoholism, other drugs, HIV infection, etc.

If your students are seriously taken with psychoanalytic theory, they might like to try out psychoanalytic re-enactments of the "birth trauma" using cushions etc. (This exercise is rumoured to work well in California.)

Set the students into groups, and ask each group to collect three examples of different cultural infant-rearing practices.

Teamwork is a good way of contrasting biological, maturational, environmental, cognitive and social factors in development. Ask each of the different teams to use one of these perspectives to account for the changes within the infant's world.

Ask your students to list some of the problems of undertaking research on babies, and in particular, to examine how psychologists have tried to overcome the babies' lack of language.

Students can list how babies communicate to allow a discussion of the interactive nature of communication. Try making comparisons with animal communication.

Get your students to appraise the whole topic of infant development in terms of ethical issues, bringing out examples of research methods, findings and applications which might have ethical implications.

Early childhood

You might want to introduce key figures in developmental psychology by dividing the students into groups, and asking them to undertake research on Piaget, Vygotsky, Freud, and Bowlby before feeding back the information to the whole class.

Alternatively, the range of theories of linguistic development can be explored by asking different student groups to focus on the strengths and weaknesses of the theories of language development formulated by Chomsky, Piaget, Bruner and Vygotsky.

To introduce Chomsky's approach, try putting a sentence up on the board and asking the students to analyse the sentence structure (e.g. phonemes, morphemes, semantic and syntactical rules).

The BPS audio tape produced by Louise Higgins is an excellent classroom device for illustrating linguistic development.

The topic of play can be introduced by getting your students to reminisce about the games they used to play as children. Why do they think they gave up playing games like tag, hide and seek, and so on?

This can also lead into discussions about siblings in family play, and how valid studies of play which only look at age-stratified groups really are.

The function of games can be raised by discussing the role of adult games such as Trivial Pursuit, pool, or charades.

Explore gender socialisation by getting students to perform a content analysis on early "readers" such as Ladybird books published in the 1960s and 1970s. Compare these with the content of contemporary books.

Gender role socialisation can also be explored by looking at the images in TV advertising. Develop a coding system in class, based on categories such as initiating activity, following etc., and ask students to code adverts shown at different times of day. Are there differences in the gender roles of adverts aimed at different age groups?

Why not set up a class debate between those who support Freudian theories of gender identity and those who don't?

Make a list of Piagetian terms, and conduct a rapid-fire class quiz, asking students to define the terms quickly as you read them out.

Alternatively, duplicate the lists, set students into groups, and ask them to complete the definitions in the shortest time.

Draw up a class chart to compare various stages of early childhood development, such as vocabulary acquisition, stages of children's drawings, development of empathy, and so on.

Collect accounts of small children's remarks from parents and other family members. Do these reveal information about regularities or stages in childhood thinking?

Pick out some of the key terms used by developmental psychologists (e.g. id, ego, sensori-motor development, zone of proximal development). Get your students to link these terms with different developmental theorists, and to provide a simple definition of each one.

Middle childhood

Historical factors in developmental psychology might be explored by bringing in artists' impressions of children over the centuries, and discussing how the image and perception of children has changed.

Given the importance of schooling in Western civilisation, you might start a discussion of middle childhood by setting students into groups, asking each group to list the benefits and drawbacks of children going to school.

The students might also consider how childhood school experience relates to Erikson's stages of development, or how it may contribute to the child's transition from pre-operational to concrete operational thought.

Ask the students to collect as many cross-cultural examples of alternative forms of reasoning as they can, from a range of cultures (e.g. Brazilians, Native Australians). What implications does this have in terms of the universality of Piaget's theories?

Moral development can be introduced by asking students (preferably in groups) to list three things which make them feel guilty. If they can remember what types of things made them feel guilty as children, it might be interesting to make comparisons.

"WELL! I DON'T REALLY NEED TO ASK WHO'S RESPONSIBLE FOR THIS DO I?"

Concepts of "fairness" and equity may be explored with examples of adult cheating as well as childhood instances.

Ask the students to respond to one of Kohlberg's dilemmas, and then to evaluate each other's answers. This inevitably allows you to discuss the difficulties experienced in classifying answers to moral dilemmas, and to explore the adequacy of stage theories of this kind.

Try getting your class to invent moral dilemmas suitable for different age groups. They can use these as the basis for a practical exercise if they want.

See how many of your students can remember learning to read, and if they can, look at the method which was used to teach them. Use this to identify the psychological theory underlying the method (i.t.a., flash cards etc.). Were different theories popular at different times?

Ask about students' experiences of learning a second language, and why it seems to be different from learning one's own language. Explore different factors, such as early experience, travel etc.

It's often interesting to ask students who didn't learn to recite tables at school how they solve multiplication sums in their head (e.g. 7 × 6), to demonstrate alternative strategies for arithmetical reasoning.

The study of intelligence is always made more interesting by giving students examples of intelligence test items to try, and then discussing whether they think such questions measure intelligence. Be careful though, of your students' self-esteem. For this reason, it is best not to use whole tests or give general scores.

A good general summarising exercise when students are coming near to the end of their study of child development is to write the headings "social", "intellectual", "emotional" and "physical" development on the board, and ask students to list how they have changed in these areas over the years.

Adolescence

Try beginning a discussion of adolescence by asking your students to list the tasks of this period of life (e.g. career decisions, relationship decisions, etc.). It may be best to do this as a group exercise, and to compare the outcomes from each group. Then ask them to divide the final list into two: ones which are different from their parents'/grandparents' generation, and ones which are the same.

Set students into groups and ask them to find instances of cross-cultural social practices based around the physical changes of adolescence. For example, the age of consent for sexual intercourse differs in different countries; in Belgium, some girls celebrate the onset of menstruation with a party, and so on.

Follow this up by asking the students to list markers of their own transitions from childhood to adolescence such as the first purchase of a bra, some make up, or a CD. You might like to get your students to explore the idea of exams as the initiation rites of our own society.

Ideal body image can be explored by devising an "identikit" body made from strips of card with different diameters of waist, hips etc. Ask students to devise the ideal body shape for various categories (e.g. my ideal self; what they think a young man's preferred girlfriend would be like; what they think a young woman's preferred boyfriend would be like, etc.). Ask them to summarise the findings, and see if they contrast with the literature on body image and self-esteem.

Try giving your students examples of Piagetian problems to test formal operational thought. To restore their self-esteem, you might tell them that when Wason used the same tests on modern university graduates, they found them hard too. Ask them to explore reasons why modern adolescents might find these tests harder than Piaget's adolescents did.

Alternatively, ask your students how they feel their moral development has changed over the years, or whether they use different strategies when they are trying to persuade someone to accept their point of view.

You might want to raise the role of the media in terms of how it constructs youth identity (e.g. youth as rebel, problem, drop-out) as well as discussing its contribution to gender identity. This allows you to discuss possible causes of anorexia, too.

To explore different social expectations, try getting your students to collect newspaper articles about adolescents, and also newspaper articles featuring children.

Get them to bring in problem pages from adolescent magazines, and classify the types of problems. They might like to contrast this with some equivalent adult magazines.

Using Erikson's stages of development as a framework, ask students to write down the real-life problems they believe to be typical of each stage. How closely do their ideas match Erikson's?

Ask your students to consider whether adolescence is more stressful than other periods of life. This allows you to discuss avoidable and unavoidable stress. If you have mature students in the class, you may find that their views differ, and if there are enough, you may be able to set up a class debate on the subject. Be careful not to polarise the class, though.

Development in adulthood

One excellent starting point for this topic is to write the words "Grown-up" on the board, and ask students to discuss what constitutes being a grown-up (e.g. age, responsibilities, employment, partnerships, parenthood). List their ideas, and then ask them to make comparisons with Levinson's stages of adulthood or Gould's, to see if they correspond.

It is also interesting to ask students to explore the notion of being "on time" or "late"' for developmental tasks. First, ask the students to list as many developmental tasks as they possibly can (leaving college, getting a job, forming a long-term relationship, becoming a parent etc.). Setting them into groups to do this is a good idea.

Once you have a fairly lengthy list, ask each group to identify the "appropriate" age for each developmental task. Compare the answers from each group—did they all reach the same conclusions? If you have an evening class and a daytime one, you may like to see whether different-aged students tend to give different responses.

A possible follow-up to this is to ask the groups to draw up a chart listing biological, social and economic factors that might influence such decisions within a range of cultures.

Life-events can be explored in a variety of ways. Many teachers use Holmes and Rahe's Social Readjustment Rating Scale as a starting point. Alternatively, you may like to encourage your class to develop their own scale, beginning by writing lists of all of the stressful life-events they can think of. They can allocate a score for each event, perhaps working from the baseline information that marriage was given a rating of 50 (initially 500) in the Holmes and Rahe scale. This exercise also allows you to discuss the use of numerical values for life-events.

Try putting up a set of descriptions taken from Holmes and Rahe such as marriage, divorce, redundancy, or the death of spouse. Ask students to consider how these events would affect or change their lives. However, do be careful when you are discussing stressful life-events, since almost inevitably at least one of your students will be in the middle of one.

Another way of tackling this is to separate the students into pairs, and to ask each pair to investigate different stressful life-events—major ones, like parenting, marriage, death or divorce. Ask them to find and report back on psychological research on the topic.

Get your students to bring magazine articles on "How my life changed" into class. Use these to explore some of the factors that contribute to change in adulthood.

Begin the topic of ageing by setting up a group brainstorming session for the term "old age". Then divide the board into a "positive" and a "negative" column, and see how many of the outcomes fit in each column.

Ask your students to list the social, cognitive and physical changes they expect to occur in old age. Having listed such expectations they can then consider whether the changes are an inevitable aspect of ageing, or whether they are the result of cultural factors (e.g. retirement at 65).

Try setting up a classroom debate between those who see ageing as an inevitable and rapid decline into senility, and those who see it in a more positive way. Ask each side to produce psychological evidence to support its argument.

Another way of looking at ageism is to get the students to bring in stories from local newspapers about older people. These invariably stereotype the elderly. You might like to contrast these with case studies, such as Nelson Mandela becoming a prime minister at the age of 75, which challenge such stereotyping.

The topic of ageing also allows you to explore gender difference and prejudice. For instance, women having children in their late 50s are perceived as "going against nature" whilst males fathering children at this age are often perceived quite differently.

Set your students into groups, and ask each group to list the advantages and dis-advantages of living to the age of 200. Did each group identify the same set?

INDIVIDUAL DIFFERENCES

Intelligence & intelligence testing

A good way of beginning this subject is to ask the students to give you some definitions of intelligence. You might want to discuss exam performance, sporting achievements, quiz show success, or brilliant robberies to pull out the cultural values implicit in defining intelligence.

Try asking students to list abilities which they consider contribute to their labelling someone as "intelligent". See whether they match Thurstone's, or whether they can be fitted into Guilford's "cube" model. If the students find it difficult to reach a consensus, try getting them to identify the factors which would lead them to conclude that someone was stupid.

One of the best ways of tackling the nature–nurture debate is to organise a classroom debate. Get half of the group to look for evidence of intelligence as inherited, while the other half looks for evidence as learned. Organise the debate formally, with speakers for each side, summing up, and the like.

Having established that intelligence is a controversial topic you could broach the problem of trying to measure it, by asking the students to devise questions to see if a 5-year-old and a 10-year-old child were intelligent.

Get students to list the advantages and disadvantages of IQ tests. Again, they could do this in teams, as a formal debate if you like.

Ask students, in groups, to produce reasoned *psychological* responses to different questions, such as:

- should people with higher IQs be sent to different schools?
- should people who confess to numerous crimes be given IQ tests to evaluate the usefulness of their confessions?
- to what extent is an absent-minded professor more intelligent than a practical plumber?

Have some established tests at hand (if nothing else is available, get a couple from H.J. Eysenck's "Know your own IQ" books). Ask your students how they would ascertain whether the tests were reliable or valid.

A word of warning, though: avoid getting students to do intelligence tests in class individually, since it can contribute greatly to feelings of insecurity. Even when the intention is to examine problems in questionnaire design or practice, students often feel themselves to be failures if they can't answer the questions. Rather than use the tests individually, you can give groups of students a range of questions and ask them what they think the test is measuring. You can also allow groups of students to collaborate on answers.

When looking at tests , you might also get students to discuss what they think has been left out. This can introduce the idea of creativity and creativity tests. Try students on the "uses for a brick" test, and discuss the answers with them. When you've done that, try them on "uses for a paper clip". It's interesting to see how, once they are aware that the more bizarre the answers, the more creative they are thought to be, their answers change.

Approach Gardner's theory by telling students about the idea that there are different kinds of intelligence, and asking them to develop their own list of what those kinds might be. See if they come up with the same set.

Personality: Factor theories

One starting point to personality is to get the students to think of someone they like or dislike, and describe them. This should enable you to pull out some of the terms people commonly use to describe personality. Depending on what students say, it also might lead you into discussions about the difference between behaviour and traits.

An alternative is to get them to write personality descriptions of each other, and see how easy it is for them to recognise themselves and each other from those descriptions. But this isn't the kind of thing you should use for a new class—rather, one in which a good rapport had already been established within the group. It's important that people don't find it too intrusive. A less threatening variant of the same method would be to ask them to describe the personality of someone from a well-known TV soap, to see if the others can guess who it is.

Distinction between trait and type approaches can be explored by asking students to list as many traits as they can think of, and then grouping together the ones they think go together, e.g. "shy" and "reserved". When they are looking at these groupings, they can often find it easier to see how traits are descriptions of what is to be found within the individual, while types are descriptions that the individual is expected to fit into.

This can lead you into some interesting discussions about the Barnum Effect, and horoscopes—which are, after all, the most widely-accepted type theories of personality in everyday life. Don't be surprised to find your students deeply sceptical about extroversion, but showing total belief in astrological types!

Demonstrate the Barnum Effect using general plausible horoscope readings from magazines, without identifying names. Ask students to rate privately, on a scale of one to five, how far each of a set of readings applies to them personally. Presenting the readings singly at intervals during the session, and doing other work in between, often makes the effect even stronger.

Discussions about whether personality is consistent over time and situations can be opened out by asking students whether they

think they have changed during their lives. This might also lead you into discussions of how life events and personality change, for example by discussing people who survive traumatic experiences. Get students to look at specific cases, such as that of Simon Weston of the Falklands War, to explore whether this affects personality. Situational specificity can be explored by inviting students to consider how they would be likely to act in a number of named situations. You could also try getting them to list situations in which it would actually help them to know someone's personality type, and explain what form that help would take.

You'll probably find that opinions in the class differ between those who see personality types as useful, and those who don't. Try setting this up as a formal debate, with speakers for each side (5 minutes each, max.), and a vote at the end.

Most students enjoy taking and criticising personality tests, so try to get some examples of well-known personality questionnaires. Get them to look at the questions and say what they think each question is trying to measure. This can lead you into some useful discussions about validity, reliability and standardisation norms. If you have any sets of population norms for the test, you could try getting them to guess what the norms for any given trait might be, before telling them the answers.

Alternatively, approach questions of validity and reliability by getting your students into groups and asking them to devise five questions for measuring specific traits. It's often very interesting to take introversion and neuroticism and see what they come up with. The groups can then report back to the class and critically discuss the questions. You might also ask the groups to consider how they would detect if someone were lying.

If you have any available, give students a TAT picture to look at, or devise one of your own. This allows you to explore how projective tests differ from rating scales and personality inventories. If the students are willing to write stories to the pictures you could get the class to discuss the various interpretations that could be given. As a last resort, get students to construct some ink-blots, in the time-honoured way (very popular, this one) and ask them to develop scoring keys by collecting interpretations.

Cognitive approaches to personality

The easiest way into this topic is to lead the students into how each of these three cognitive approaches to personality can be applied in understanding their own lives. Approach personal construct therapy by inviting students to complete a simplified repertory grid. Then they can compare one another's grids, to compare some of the different dimensions which have come up as constructs. If you think this would be too personally threatening for students in your particular group, it is possible to look at it by comparing constructs about artefacts, or about well-known people or groups in society. Get them to draw up rep grids on the basis of makes of cars, for example, or different TV characters, rather than on the basis of their own close relationships. It should still produce interesting differences in personal constructs, and can also lead you into some useful discussions of the problems involved in the method.

Rogers' model can be explored by asking students to generate "I am" statements. This is best done in groups—again, it minimises any personal threat which individuals might feel. The difference between self and ideal-self can be discussed in terms of which statement best describes the person as they are now, and which describes the person as they would like to be.

Another interesting exercise is to get students to attempt to be entirely non-directive in conversation. The best way to approach this is in triads, with one person being the "counsellor", one being the "client", and one observing and taking notes. Keep them away from very personal topics, but get the "counsellors" to elicit conversation about things like hobbies, favourite college subjects, how they approach exams, preparing for birthdays, etc.

To introduce Bandura's idea of self-efficacy, you can ask the students about any areas of life that they think that they are no good at, and then explore why. This often raises questions about their experiences at school. Alternatively you can ask them about any area of their lives that they feel they are successful in. From their examples you should be able to discuss vicarious experiences, social persuasion and emotional arousal.

You could try doing role-play of the therapeutic situation with the students, but only with students who enjoy them. Rogerian therapy particularly lends itself to this. One student can role-play the therapist, while the other plays the client. Try giving the "client" a slip of paper with a particular personal problem written on it. Do this with three or four pairs, and then get the group to discuss how easy (or otherwise) it is to communicate unconditional positive regard, and to be genuine, empathic and warm.

The question of whether positive regard is something you would always want from everyone can be explored by asking students to list any circumstances in which they feel better because someone dislikes them (for example, would you really want to be approved of by a member of the National Front?). You could also discuss whether there are any circumstances in which they would find it hard to give someone else unconditional positive regard. What would they do if Hitler came for counselling?

To introduce Bandura's idea of self-efficacy, try asking the students to list ten things that they are good at. These might be as trivial as the ability to make nice mashed potato, or more significant, like having a Silver Medal in Lifesaving. Getting people to read out their lists can often reveal unknown hobbies and interests. It can also lead you into discussions about Bandura's argument that it is better to have higher self-efficacy beliefs than the evidence might actually warrant, and from there into the whole question of how self-efficacy beliefs influence effort and achievement.

You also might try asking the students about any areas of life that they think they are no good at, and then explore why. This often raises questions about their experiences at school, and you can lead the discussion into ideas about self-fulfilling prophecies, modelling, and attributions.

Before and after shots in slimming and/or body building magazines can also be used to explore issues of personality change and whether we take on other people's definition of ourselves.

To pull these cognitive theories together, try giving the students a case study of someone's behaviour and asking different groups to adopt a different theoretical perspective. Each group would then show how each of the cognitive models would explain it, and suggest appropriate strategies for helping that individual.

Approaches to abnormality

WARNING!!! Do take care when you are teaching this subject. Students often think their psychology teacher can help them if they have personal problems, or a member of their family is acting strangely. If this situation arises, don't get drawn into things, but do advise them to seek professional help—or at the very least, a qualified counsellor.

Also, be tactful! Always assume that someone in the class, or a member of their family etc. has been labelled mentally ill, whether you know about it or not.

A good starting point to discuss abnormality is to put the two words "normal"

and "abnormal" on the board and brainstorm the associations associated with the word. More subtly, try dividing the students into groups, giving each group a slip of paper with either "normal" or "abnormal" on it, and asking them to produce 20 words associated with the one they have.

These techniques allow you to raise all sorts of interesting issues, such as whether the two words really are opposite in meaning to one another, and whether normality involves more judgements about social acceptability than abnormality, or vice versa.

Another starting point is to bring in a selection of case studies and ask the students to read them and discuss what they think is wrong with the person being described, if anything, and how it could be sorted out.

Try getting students into groups, and asking each group to describe seven features of abnormality. See what the different groups' results have in common, and then compare them with Rosenhan and Seligman's features of abnormality.

Alternatively, try using Rosenhan and Seligman's seven features of abnormality as the starting point, and ask the students to think of counter-examples.

Get students to bring in examples of the use of the words "abnormal" and "normal" in newspaper and popular magazine articles. What do the words actually mean, when they are used in these contexts? And what are they being used to indicate?

One of the interesting questions here is how far instances of "irrational" behaviour have their counterparts in our everyday experience. Try inviting students to think of everyday equivalents to "abnormal" behaviours—like suddenly saying something aloud while rehearsing an argument mentally.

The role of context in interpreting behaviour as abnormal can be introduced by asking your more extrovert students to act out a number of scenes, like "being at a disco" or "having lunch in a cafeteria". Try giving the audience a wrong description of what is supposed to be happening—so that what they see is inappropriate behaviour for the context—and see how they respond. Alternatively, get two students to act out conflicting scenes together, so that one is, say, a doctor being consulted by a patient, while the other is trying to chat someone up at a disco. It can get very funny, but it also makes some interesting points.

Keep an eye open for TV programmes exploring mental illness. Documentaries about the social effects of "care in the community" policies, or crime and mental illness provide you with useful material to discuss the question of distinctions between abnormality and normality, and whether some people need special forms of social and emotional support.

Forms of pathology

CAUTION!!! You will need to warn the students that reading about the various mental disorders doesn't necessarily mean that they are suffering from the whole range of ailments available. Take care that teaching this subject doesn't just become an invitation to irresponsible self-diagnosis, or, worse still, amateur diagnosis of friends and family.

A good starting point for teaching psychopathology is to give students the range of disorders (e.g. paranoid schizophrenia, personality disorders etc.) and to get them to find out as much as they can about each set. Try putting them into groups, and giving each group one set of disorders to find out about. Then they can report back to the rest of the class.

Ask your students to think up case descriptions, and ask the others to identify the diagnostic category which is being described. If several people think up their own case descriptions for each category, you should be able to make some interesting teaching points about lack of homogeneity in diagnostic categories, leading to questions about validity and reliability, etc.

Alternatively, the use of case studies can highlight the differences between the range of disorders, rather than within the categories themselves.

The five axes of DSM-III-R can also be explored by using a case study. You might choose someone prominent in the media, such as David Icke or Michael Winner, and look at how he—or at least his public image—might be interpreted in terms of the five axes. When discussing personality disorders, ask the students to write down a list of five factors which they consider contribute to anti-social behaviour. How many of them correspond to the established definitions of the anti-social personality? Follow this up by asking the students how many of these factors they have seen manifested by public figures.

Try having a classroom debate on questions like: "Is 'Beadle's About' simply a showcase for the psychopathic personality?" With luck, opinions should be fairly well divided in the class, and you could get a good debate going. Have speakers for each case, giving them plenty of time to prepare their arguments, and round it off with a vote at the end.

The use of drugs in treating mental disorders can be discussed by giving the students a list of the main drugs available and asking them to find out what the drugs are given for, what their side effects are, what psychiatrists are trying to do when prescribing them, and what physical effects they produce in the brain. Draw up a chart, with the names of the drugs for the rows, and these questions for the columns. Hand them to small groups of students, and ask them to complete them as a group, using books in the library or elsewhere. Then compare the answers in class.

There's also material for a classroom debate on the nature–nurture debate on schizophrenia or depression. Divide the class into two groups and get them to choose speakers who will put forward the case for either genetic theory or the environmental (family) theory. By polarising the issues in this way (make sure you pick people for each side who already believe in what they are arguing) you can round off the debate by presenting the vulnerability model. You can also raise questions about what kinds of evidence seem to be most appropriate, and how evidence is gathered.

There are numerous films that explore the area of mental illness, such as *Rain Man*, *Awakenings*, *One Flew Over the Cuckoo's Nest*, *A Clockwork Orange*, etc. One of the best films for really getting students to think about mental illness and the process of labelling is Ken Loach's film *Family Life*, which is definitely worth trying to get hold of on video, to show students in class.

Therapeutic approaches

One starting point for discussing therapeutic approaches is to ask the students what type of help they would seek if they were suffering from periods of severely disordered thinking, or a severe phobia which meant they couldn't lead their ordinary lives, or a personality disorder which made it difficult to get on with other people. This should allow you to explore the distinction between understanding behaviour (i.e. why you do something) and changing it.

The behaviourist approach can be explored in the classroom by getting the students to collect examples of classical and operant conditioning from everyday life. For example,

"... IT'S FOR YOUR OWN GOOD MR. LIDFLIP... YOU'LL THANK ME FOR THIS..."

how they feel ill if a certain food is mentioned, if they were once ill after eating it. This leads you into discussions about whether this type of learning is under conscious control or not. Ask the students to provide a list of reinforcements that they think might provide a change in their behaviour.

You might also ask the students to create anxiety hierarchies, e.g. for a fear of spiders, and to describe how someone using systematic desensitisation might approach the problem gradually.

You can explore the use of reinforcements in class by getting the students to smile and look interested whenever you are in one part of the room and to look bored when you move to another part. What effect does it have on you? Does it make a difference if you know what they are doing?

This can also lead you into discussions about the ethics of manipulating people without their consent, and about questions of freedom of choice in the case of the psychiatric patient. Try setting up a classroom debate on this one.

To explore the relevance of research on animals to humans, simply write the word "rat" on one side of the board and "human" on the other and ask them to list the differences between the two species. To get it a bit more structured, ask small groups to devise a list of 10 behavioural similarities and 10 differences. Did each group get the same set? Were there disagreements within the groups themselves?

Techniques of psychoanalysis can be explored by giving the students a free-association task to do. Give them words like "mother", "brother", "life" and "sex" and ask them to write down the first five words that come into their minds. If you want to stay off the heavy Freudian stuff, try Jungian words like "sea", "mountain", "sun", "father" etc. Look at questions like whether students' responses are affected by culture, and whether there are individual differences in responses.

If you feel confident, you can get the students to recall a particular dream and attempt an analysis using Freudian techniques. Focus on symbolism and free-association to images or objects in the dream. Be careful, though, because some students can take all this very seriously indeed.

Cognitive therapy can be introduced by asking the students to explain any failures that they might have experienced, such as a failed exam, a failed driving test or a bad date. It is useful to give them some examples from your own history so that they realise that failing is part of life. Their answers can then be looked at in terms of errors in logic, of the sort which might be identified by a rational-emotive therapist.

Alternatively you could ask them what advice a cognitive psychologist might give them if they expressed anxiety about failing their A level exam, and how this would be different from the advice that a cognitive therapist might give.

To contrast the different schools, take an example of a specific disorder and get the students to research how different theorists would attempt to explain it. Try something like, say, a fear of cats which has become so extreme that the person won't leave their house. Divide the students into groups and ask each group to put forward a different perspective. Ask them to explain how the disorder came about, and what the treatment should be. You could have more than one group taking the same theory, and see how similar their ideas are.

BIOPSYCHOLOGY

The nervous system
A starting point for discussing the nervous system could be to ask each student to shake hands with the person next to them, and then to ask them what was involved in such an action. You can use this at first to link biopsychology with other areas of psychology

(social, cognitive etc.), and then steer the discussion towards the physiological mechanisms involved: sight, hearing, muscle co-ordination, etc.

Gapped handouts are always a useful way of inviting students to recall crucial names and structures, but do remember to be prepared to negotiate a bit: students often come up with answers which weren't the ones you had in mind when you wrote the handout, but which do make sense in the context of the subject. While it's perfectly reasonable to expect them to know what subject they are studying (e.g. sociological answers not acceptable), it's not really fair to penalise them for failing to be telepathic!

Ask students to make sets of paired cards, where one card gives the part of the nervous system and the other gives its function. You can do this as a class exercise, or you can set the class into two teams and get each team to develop 25 pairs of cards. Shuffle the cards well, give them to the opposite team, start the teams off together and see which team finishes matching them up first.

Collect case studies of people who have suffered from brain injury. Put them on the OHP, one at a time, and ask your students to examine the symptoms to see if they can deduce what parts of the brain were probably involved. You might also ask them to explain the origins of other well-known disorders which appear in the textbooks, such as Parkinson's disease, Korsakoff's syndrome, agnosia etc.

Ask the students to name as many psychoactive drugs as they can. The list can include common legal drugs such as caffeine, nicotine and alcohol as well as illegal ones. Develop a final list and then set the students into groups and ask them to find out how these drugs influence neurotransmission in the brain. If you like, the groups can choose different drugs, but make sure each group has at least two, and preferably three to investigate. Also, make sure that any one drug

is being investigated by at least two groups since one group may turn up details the other has missed.

This area lends itself well to classroom quizzes. Divide the students into small groups (teams) of about five or six members each. Give each team time to write 20 or 25 different questions, and then conduct the quiz by getting each team, in turn, to ask five questions. Give each team two turns, so that there are ten questions per team in total (the additional questions are so that they have spares when another team uses their questions). Tot up the points, giving team members 10 marks to start with for their own questions. It's up to you whether you ask who had the highest marks on an individual basis, or whether you ask teams to total their marks and see which was the winning team.

If you want to join in and ask your ten questions as well, why not develop a set of visual questions, using OHP acetates? For example, show an OHP of different EEG patterns and see if students can label them, or a picture of the cerebral cortex with just one area picked out in colour, which they have to name.

More dramatically-inclined/imaginative students may like to invent charade-like ways of portraying different parts of the nervous system in terms of their functions. For example, they might like to act out a sensory neurone carrying information quickly from A to B, a motor neurone rushing an impulse from the CNS to move a part of the body, or a frontal lobe making a decision, etc. The rest of the class can either guess the function, or if that proves too difficult, award marks for the performance.

Develop a methodology chart, listing different ways of studying the brain in the columns, and different areas of the brain in the rows (cerebrum, medulla, cerebellum, etc.). Enter on the chart all the studies you can find, which have helped us to understand how the brain works. You might want to list the four lobes of the cerebral cortex separately for this one.

Language, hemisphere function & memory

To introduce this topic, write a word on the board, and ask your students to explain how they can read and understand it. This enables you to discuss visual pathways, the visual cortex and the angular gyrus as well as Broca's and Wernicke's areas. It also allows you to link this in with wider areas, such as development (learning to read), culture (understanding the language), and cognition (understanding the concept underlying the word).

Try giving students a list of behaviours, such as reading words, perceptions of faces and pictures, telling others about our feelings, listening to music), and asking them to identify which hemisphere is thought to dominate in each activity.

Write a simple sentence on the board, and ask students to copy it down with their "other" hand, the one they don't usually write with. Since some will be able to do it much more easily than others, this can be used to discuss how handedness varies in its extent from one person to another. You can also demonstrate that the decision as to which hemisphere is dominant is not always easy to ascertain by asking the students which hand or foot they perform particular activities with.

Looking at another person through a tube held out at arm's length is a useful indicator of eye dominance. The eye which the other person can see looking at them is the dominant one.

Develop a list of ten physical activities such as kicking a ball, crossing one arm over the other, stepping out into the road, spooning the last custard out of a saucepan, etc. Read the list out very quickly and ask students to jot down either R or L, according to which hand or foot they think they would use. Don't give them time to think about it. Then, ask them to act out the activity. Was there a difference when they actually performed the action?

Students might also want to think about some of the linguistic connotations associated with the term "left" (two left feet, sinister etc.). You might also mention that parrots are exclusively left-clawed in that they perch on their right foot and hold food in their left. They might also like to consider how psychologists found this out.

The physiology of learning and memory can sometimes be looked at in terms of the student's own experiences. While few may have experienced a blow on the head, some may have experienced loss of memory due to an excess of alcohol, or have elderly relatives who are experiencing difficulties with memory. It's a good starting point for discussion.

To continue, try asking your class to give you examples of different types of learning and remembering used by both humans and animals, and list them on the board. Try organising these into types such as autobiographical memories, geographical knowledge, memories of skills, and so on. Once you have done this, ask the students to find out which of these types of memory have been studied in terms of their physiological mechanisms. They might also like to identify types of memory which have been left out.

Research into learning and memory raises ethical questions about animal experimenta-tion. Get your students to collect examples of animal experiments in this area, and to evaluate them in ethical terms. Were they all unacceptable, all acceptable, or are some more unacceptable than others?

Try listing a number of biochemical substances involved in memory, e.g. acetylcholine, thiamine, dopamine etc. Set your students into small groups and ask the groups to find out about the function of each of these substances. Give all groups the same list, since some will produce fuller accounts than others.

The study of research into transfer of knowledge through ingestion of brain substance could be enlivened by asking students whose brain they would most like to consume if knowledge could be transferred in this way. Be aware, though, that this discussion invariably leads one student to ask why they don't remember a sheep's experiences even though they have eaten sheep's brains.

Set your students into groups, and ask each group to imagine that they are a team of research scientists who are trying to find out whether the ingestion process could work for human beings. They have to find an *ethical* way of investigating this. (Note: Don't worry if they conclude that it's impossible. Failure in this task leads you into interesting discussions about social responsibility of science, whether ends justify means, or whether some things are just forbidden knowledge, and so on.)

Stress, anxiety & emotion

One way of beginning this area is to ask students to list five situations which have caused them stress, and to ask them to describe the physical feelings which they feel when they are in those situations: muscular tension, increased heart rate, etc. Ask the students to notice particularly whether there are differences in the feelings produced by short-term stress (e.g. being late for an important appointment) and long-term stress (e.g. the build-up to exams). This provides a way of introducing the similarities and differences between the fight or flight reaction (short-term) and the general adaptation syndrome (long-term).

Set your students into small groups, and ask each group to produce a list of the advantages and disadvantages of stress.

Put the Holmes and Rahe stressful life-events on cards, so that each card in a set lists just one stressful life-event. Ask the students to sort the cards in rank order, from most stressful to least stressful. Working in groups is good for this one, but it means you need more than one set of cards. If you like, the groups can also assign point values to the events, but make sure that they use the same range and mid-point (50) as the original. Then compare their conclusions with the actual scale. Use any differences which emerge to investigate questions like whether there are differences between populations (e.g. students as opposed to executives), whether times have changed since 1974 and the scale has become obsolete; and whether there are events which you underestimate unless you have been through them, such as the loss of a loved partner or parent.

Some students may have had some kind of stress-related problem in the past (eczema, asthma etc.) Don't pry, but it's worth asking if anyone has experienced anything which they can now see was a reaction to the stress of that time. If any are willing to talk about it, encourage your students to look for the sources of stress which may have provoked the disorder, and at the feelings which those sources evoked. Spend some time, too, discussing positive coping strategies which might have presented an alterative. Don't do this with current problems, though. Amateur diagnosis in the classroom is much too risky, not to mention unethical!

If you know the group well and they enjoy that sort of thing, you could give them a series of questions to see if they are Type A personalities. Also, ask the group to rank each other in terms of who they consider is the most like a Type A personality and who they consider the least like a Type A, and compare the outcomes. Don't risk this if any members of the group are unwilling, though, because it can be seen as an intrusion into someone's personal privacy.

To see if students understand the basic principles of coping with stress, you could ask them to write a magazine article giving advice to people on how to cope with stress, or to devise a plan of action which might be included in something like a health education leaflet.

Ask your students to scan newspapers, magazines, leaflets in doctors' waiting rooms etc. for advice on stress, and bring it all into

WHEN FACED WITH ANXIETY, PHYLLIS WOULD ALWAYS ACT PROMPTLY.

class. Then sort out the different recommendations in terms of what aspect of the stress response the advice is tackling. Use categories such as "changing the physiological condition", "challenging negative beliefs", "developing an internal locus of control" etc.

Set your students into groups and ask each group to develop a set of five practical recommendations which they personally might adopt to reduce exam stress. Expect them also to be able to show the psychological (or physiological) basis for their recommendation, such as to take vigorous exercise because it uses the adrenalin positively and allows parasympathetic activity afterwards, etc. Warn them that you will be expecting them to put their own advice into practice come exam time!

Sleep, arousal & motivation

Since most of your students will have gone without sleep at some time, a good way of starting this topic is to ask how this affected their behaviour, and how long it took them to catch up on the sleep that they missed. How do their experiences compare with the symptoms reported from sleep-deprivation studies?

Draw up columns on the board, headed "behavioural measures", "physiological measures" and "central measures" of arousal. Ask students to complete the chart by filling in the columns.

Set your students into groups, and ask them to list all the "natural" rhythms that they can think of (e.g. the flow of the tide, the seasons, hibernation, menstruation, perhaps even

Seasonal Affective Disorder). When collecting in the results from the groups, list them under the headings of circadian, infradian and ultradian rhythms. If one list seems a bit short set them back into their groups to find examples of just that one.

If you don't mind being accused of pop psychology, try getting hold of one of those biorhythm programmes for computers (your computing department will almost certainly have one, if only for open days). Put the students into pairs, so that they each calculate their partner's biorhythms in terms of intellectual, physical and emotional peaks and troughs. You could always convert this into a practical by first asking your students to monitor how they felt on these dimensions three times a day for a fortnight, and then correlating these with the predictions of the computer programme. Beware of the Barnum Effect, though!

Jet lag is a particularly good library research topic. Set the students into groups and send them to the library to find out about it (a phone call to the librarian beforehand doesn't go amiss). During the feedback session afterwards, if you have any students who have any experience of working shifts, or who have made long-haul flights, ask them about their experiences in shifting from one time-pattern to another, and see how the personal experiences compare with the literature.

Begin the study of motivation by asking students to list six things that they do, and why they do them. Alternatively, ask them to develop a set of seven human needs, and see whether they bear any resemblance to the ones in Maslow's hierarchy.

Ask your students to monitor any TV advertisements they see during a single week. Ask them to keep a list of what the product was, and what motivational impulse the advert was trying to key into. When they have got the information, set them into groups, and

ask the groups to organise their examples into different types of motives. It's interesting to compare the categories that the different groups develop, as well as the adverts themselves.

Since hunger and thirst are the most widely researched motives, ask your students to keep a diary of what they have eaten for one day. Also ask them to keep note of any special circumstances which might have influenced them, such as being hungry after exercise and seeing an advert for a chocolate bar, etc. Use this information to introduce the students to key areas such as satiation mechanisms, the central versus peripheral factors debate, the role of homoeostasis, and the idea of eating to maintain the body's set-weight.

Set up a class "Blockbusters" game, with the names drawn from mechanisms of sleep and motivation, and the clues being their definitions, or an account of their functions (e.g. "LH: damage to this area means that an animal doesn't eat"; answer: lateral hypothalamus).

Set up a three-way classroom debate on the causes of anorexia. Have teams, one which argues for a biological cause (lesions to the lateral hypothalamus etc.), one which argues for a cognitive cause (distorted self-perception etc.), and one which argues for a social cause (revenge on parents etc.). Give them time to research their arguments and find evidence, then set it up so that each team presents their case (max. 10 minutes each) and has a chance to sum up after the other cases have been presented (max. 5 minutes). At the end, take a general class vote.

Sensory information processing

To help students to learn about the different sensory systems, try putting together a set of cards which list parts of the brain involved in processing sensory information (superior colliculus, somatosensory cortex, olfactory bulb etc.). Ask groups of students to sort the cards, so that the correct bits of the brain belong to the correct sensory system—and are arranged in the correct order!

TV advertisements can only use vision and sound, even when they are trying to sell products on the basis of taste, smell and touch. So how do they deal with this problem? Divide your class into three teams, one for taste, one for smell and one for touch. Ask each team member to keep a record of all the TV adverts they see dealing with their team's topic (taste, smell, touch). A week later, give the teams 10 minutes or so to discuss the adverts they have seen, and ask them to choose five examples which tackle the problem in different ways. Then they can report back to the class as a whole.

The classic activity for investigating touch sensitivity, of course, is to take a pair of dividers (as found in the average geometry set) and a blindfold. The blindfolded person has to say whether they can feel two points of the dividers pressing their skin lightly, or just one. Different parts of the body are more sensitive than others: the dividers may be quite wide apart on the upper arm but still perceived as one stimulus, and quite close together on the fingertip but still perceived as two. You can relate this to shape of the somatosensory homunculus.

Ask your students to write down (or tell you) all the different types of pain that they have ever experienced. Include brief descriptions of how it felt as well as causes. Look over the list, and classify the responses into different categories, representing different types of pain. Then get your students to look at the physiological processes of pain, and see if they can relate their list to what is known about pain mechanisms.

Give your students a list of different types of everyday pains: a nettle sting, a small burn, a paper cut, a twisted ankle, etc., and ask your students what they usually do to reduce the pain felt on these occasions. See if any of their suggestions can be linked with the pain mechanisms which they have studied.

Ask your students to be on the lookout for newspaper or magazine articles which describe people managing extraordinary achievements while suffering serious injury. Make a collage of these on the wall of your teaching room, or on a display board (good for an open day, this one, particularly if you include a description of pain perception and a diagram, too).

Try starting the topic of smell by discussing how easily smells can bring back memories. You might then link this with a discussion of how olfactory pathways are different from those of other senses, bypassing the thalamus but connecting directly with the limbic system.

Arrange the classroom so that desks etc. form a regular grid and set your students into pairs. One pair will wear a blindfold, while the other will call from different points of the room. How accurately can the blindfolded individual pinpoint their position? And does it matter whether the caller is in front, behind, or at an angle? If you can get hold of a hearing aid, it is worth doing this activity twice, to illustrate the difference between normal hearing and artificially amplified sound. Try the hearing aid variation first, and have it turned up fairly high.

Ask the students to write down one risk or danger for each major sense (including proprioception), which would arise if that sense was completely missing. Pool the answers in a general class discussion.

Students could use food colouring to colour familiar drinks (e.g. an orange-coloured blackcurrant-flavoured drink). Ask people to taste them and judge what flavour they are—do they get it right? To see the extent of the influence of vision, they could see if people are more accurate when blindfolded.

A variant on this one is to block the sense of smell by holding the nose, or using a clothespeg, then ask people to taste pieces of potato, apple and onion. Can they tell the difference purely by taste alone, or do we need our other senses too?

COMPARATIVE PSYCHOLOGY

The basis of behaviour

A good starting point for comparative psychology is to show students part of a video of a wildlife programme but with the sound turned down. Look for a programme with sequences of animals interacting with one another, and invite students to record and characterise the behaviour which they are seeing. This can raise issues about how to observe and describe animal behaviour, as well as the difficulties involved in analysing the functions of behaviour.

Alternatively, open up your study of inherited behaviour by asking students to list what criteria they personally would use to see whether a given example of behaviour was innate. This makes a good staged group-work exercise. Begin by asking them to list the general points. Then give them a set of specific examples of animal behaviour, ideally by video if you can and critically evaluate methods used to assess why ducklings follow their mother, why fox cubs engage in rough-and-tumble play, why emperor penguins incubate a single egg on their foot, etc. Ask them to apply their general points to that particular behaviour. Then see how many of their points coincide with those of the major theorists, and finally ask them to apply the theorists' criteria to the examples.

This may lead you into discussions about the difference between an instinct, and instinctive behaviour. The usual distinction is that instincts are goal-directed (an instinct for something) but don't actually describe what the animal does, so they are no longer regarded as a useful concept.

Ask the students to devise a quiz which involves matching sign stimuli with behaviour patterns, e.g. red spots on beak, flying hawk shapes, bright red belly, which can be matched with hiding and ducking, pecking for food etc. Get groups of students to compile half a dozen questions each, and keep it for an end-of-term or revision activity.

Many of the students will have had experience of animal learning, for instance in trying to house-train dogs, or teaching pet hamsters to endure physical contact. Don't be afraid to ask them about their experiences, and to discuss them in class. Before you do so, though, make sure you discuss anthropomorphism, Lloyd Morgan's canon, and the principle of parsimony. Get the students to apply these concepts when explaining their experiences with their pets.

You might also ask them to think about whether genetics and conditioning between them are really adequate mechanisms for explaining these experiences, or whether it is necessary to invoke other mechanisms, such as cognition. It's better to keep this question for a second half of the discussion, though.

Take a few common examples of animal behaviour—such as the begging for food indulged in by some dogs, cats purring in response to being stroked, lambs returning to their mothers, etc.—set your students into groups, and ask them to apply Tinbergen's four areas of comparative psychology: development, mechanisms, function and evolution, to each one.

Key terms like fixed action patterns and consummatory stimuli can be learned by setting up a classroom quiz. Set the students into two teams, and give each team 10 minutes to devise a dozen or so questions, with a few spares in case of duplication. Then get the teams to test one another, with you as adjudicator. If you like (or if you're feeling particularly insecure on this one) you could restrict it to terms from the textbook's glossary.

Students can be encouraged to collect examples of habituation in several different species, e.g. horses not responding to the noise of traffic. You could also ask students to discuss how far certain types of animal behaviour can be changed (can you house-train a horse?).

The general application of operant conditioning can be explored by getting students to give an example of their own behaviour which they consider they learned through positive and negative reinforcement. Then try asking groups of students to think of three examples of human behaviour which they consider show that learning can take place without reinforcement. The reporting back session should lead you into discussions about the possibilities raised by behaviour shaping and secondary reinforcement, and may well provoke some interesting discussions.

Encourage students also to look for everyday applications of superstitious behaviours and learned helplessness. These can be useful in widening the scope of the learning theories of behaviourism, and also in linking this area with other areas of psychology, particularly by making connections with attribution theory, and with concepts such as locus of control and self-efficacy.

Courtship, mating & reproduction

You could introduce this topic by asking students about their own pets' courtship or reproductive behaviours. Do their cats become restless when in season; how did they act when they had kittens, etc.?

Ask students to keep an eye on wildlife documentaries on TV, and to collect examples of different courtship activities, e.g. species that pair bond for life, species that only come together for the mating season, examples of polyandry, examples of males rearing the young, and so on. They may also be able to use this to pull out some of the functions of courtship rituals.

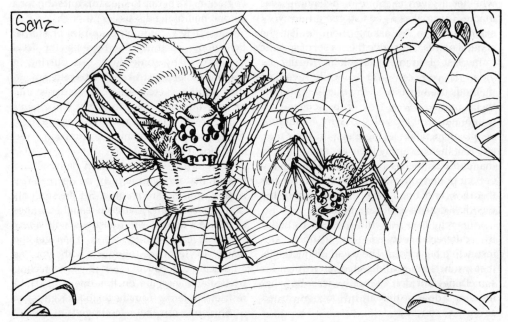

"FORGIVE ME, VERA... BUT I ALWAYS PRACTICE 'SAFE SEX'..."

While it would be unwise to encourage facile analogies, it might be worthwhile getting students to consider courtship and mating patterns of human beings. Cross-cultural research inevitably reveals wide diversity, and you can use this to encourage them to think about what this tells us, e.g., about the role of learning in human behaviour. The students might also like to consider whether operating under the somewhat restrictive fixed action patterns and sign stimuli of, say, the stickleback would make our lives a lot easier?

Try listing a few examples of different reproductive strategies—having just one youngster at a time, having a litter of half a dozen or so, producing 20 or 30 offspring, producing hundreds of offspring, producing thousands or millions. Ask students to find a species which adopts each strategy, and to consider the costs and benefits for each one. Structure the discussion around questions like whether it is more beneficial to produce many offspring that can fend for themselves early on, or to produce just one or two? And how does this relate to the amount of care and nurturing that the parents engage in?

If you want to branch off a bit you might use this to get into discussions about the possibility of cloning humans.

Take the students to a park or stream in springtime, to observe chicks following a mother duck. This can double up as an animal observation study—get them to note the behaviour of the chicks and the mother duck for a set period of about 10 minutes. Back in the classroom, you can apply theoretical work on imprinting to the observations—such as why a young duck hurries to catch up with the others when it has been left behind.

If you have a zoo nearby, you might like to arrange a visit. Encourage the students to use the concepts which they have learned, for example, by observing a primate colony and seeing if they can identify different examples of maternal behaviour, or imprinting among the hoofed mammals. A visit in springtime

usually provides some examples of courtship behaviour: a private chat beforehand with the zoo's education officer or head keeper would help you to work out the best time for such a visit.

Social organisation
One starting point for looking at social organisation is to ask the students to list animal terms which are commonly used to describe human beings, e.g. "they are just like sheep", "he's like a dog with a bone", etc. What do these comparisons tell us about our understanding of animal behaviour? And how valid are these comparisons as a means of acquiring social understanding?

You can introduce the concept of territoriality by getting students to walk up to one another and stop when they begin to feel uncomfortable. They could then discuss under what circumstances crowding can be pleasurable, e.g. rock concerts or raves, as well as looking at the techniques that they use to defend their personal space. You can go from there to look at boundary markers in human society: fences, borders and the like. In order to avoid simplistic comparisons try setting them into groups, giving each group an example of a species showing a different type of territoriality (e.g. seagulls, gibbons, chimpanzees), and asking them to list the differences between human forms of territoriality and that shown by their particular animal species.

Get the students to draw up a large wall-chart listing the common aspects of social organisation, the types of explanation which have been offered for each one, and some examples of species which have been cited as examples of each explanation.

Ask the students each to provide five examples of co-operation between animals.

Begin the topic of aggression by asking the students to write down what they understand by the word "aggression". Actually, a good way to begin this is to ask them to write down a single word which they see as its opposite. This should help them to see how the word is often used to mean many different things.

Ask the students to list different kinds of aggressive behaviour in animals. Their ideas can be matched against Moyer's classification, and you can encourage them to draw on the criticisms of this classification when discussing the result. If you intend to extend the discussion to human beings (optional), you might also raise the issue of verbal aggression, as well as the role of ritualisation in, for example, football gangs meeting each other.

It is also worthwhile getting students to look at how animals protect themselves from predators, especially the more sophisticated techniques such as letting the predator know that it has been seen, or the last-minute strategy of attracting even more predators in the hope that the victim might escape in the scuffle.

Give them a list of terms (e.g. stotting, home range, "bourgeois" strategy etc.) and ask them to write down what each term means.

The complexity of identifying dominance in any social organisation can be introduced by asking students to examine how dominance is manifest in human society. Alternatively, or in addition, get them to apply the criteria used to infer animal dominance to human behaviour: if we step aside for someone on the street, does that mean that we see them as dominant? You can go from there into the whole problem of inference in animal behaviour, if you like.

Try setting up a debate between those who believe that it is reasonable to talk of animal cognition when studying social behaviour, and those who do not.

Finally, students could be encouraged to look at how peace-making and reconciliation occurs in both humans and animals. Get them to draw out strategies mentioned in the text, and to see whether there are parallels with their own experiences of human interaction. If the students challenge you for warning them off simplistic analogies and then encouraging

them, you can justify the activity on the grounds that reconciliation is a positive, pro-social behaviour, and such simplistic analogies have usually only been made for negative or anti-social behaviours. Or you can just admit that they are right.

Communication & information

A good starting point for studying animal communication is to ask the students to list five forms of communication shown by pet animals, and what they consider the communications to mean, such as dogs wagging tails, cats miaowing, etc.

Alternatively, produce a list of modes of receiving information, e.g. smell, sight, sound, infrasound, electricity etc. and ask them to give you at least one example of animal communication using these modes. (Be warned, this is likely to get you into heated arguments about whether an electric eel is communicating with a fish when it stuns it...)

The notion that communication need not necessarily be intentional can be explored by getting students to examine non-verbal "leakage", by listing any behaviours which they consider to be real giveaways when they are trying to deceive someone, e.g. blushing, fiddling with hair, etc.

Obtain a recording of a birdsong and ask the students to try to describe it. Get them to attempt it individually, first, then set them into groups to see if they can arrive at a group consensus. Let them hear the recording as often as they like. This will lead you into discussions about the fine discrimination needed by researchers in this area (as well as by the birds themselves). If your technicians can provide you with a sound spectrograph, the students can see the different visual images produced by different bird calls.

Get the students to draw up a wall-chart with four columns representing Tinbergen's four areas of comparative psychology, and lines which represent some aspect of behaviour in a particular species, e.g. bee dances, chimpanzee facial expressions, etc.

It is also worthwhile to obtain a recording of whale songs (try the local library). Students often find these haunting and interesting to listen to, but they also raise the question of how one moves from describing com- munication to analysing its meaning.

If students are into drama you might give them some typical chimpanzee styles of communication and get them to demonstrate them in appropriate circumstances.

Alternatively, take them on a visit to your local zoo, and observe the chimpanzees there. (Note: since these animals are usually more active early in the day, try to arrange your visit for the morning, as soon as the zoo opens, if you can).

Finally, you might give the students a series of messages to convey to each other non-verbally, such as "there is a person behind you who is dangerous", or "there is some fantastic food in the next room".

Animal cognition

One good way of starting off this topic is to ask students to provide examples of animal behaviour which they consider to demonstrate animal reasoning. Before you begin, revise both Lloyd Morgan's canon and the principle of parsimony with the students, and encourage them to think of alternative explanations for the animal's behaviour. If you like, you could have a class vote on each separate item, in terms of whether it was or was not showing animal reasoning.

By asking the somewhat simple question of how does a homing pigeon "know" how to get home, you can often explore a variety of examples of student reasoning, as well as discussing how a pigeon finds its way home.

Use categories of animal cognition (imitation, curiosity, the use of cognitive maps, etc.) to devise a wall-chart, on which students can enter examples of animal behaviour seen on documentaries etc. Make sure that the chart has columns for species, the behaviour shown, the cognitive abilities which it seems to be demonstrating, the situation, and so on. Having collected the examples for a set time, such as a term, encourage students to look for regularities and structure, such as comparing species in phylogenetic terms, or seeing if primates are more likely to show certain abilities than other kinds of mammals.

One starting point for examining language training in chimps and gorillas could be to ask the students why it is difficult to train a chimpanzee to talk. With luck (and some careful steering on your part) this will encourage them to think about the different ways in which species have evolved, and why the species would have no need for vocal apparatus in the human mode.

Try obtaining a few common signs used in Ameslan or another sign language, and get the students to try to teach them to one another (including making the sign and learning its meaning) without any vocalisation. Allow the "teachers" to use the same methods used by the Gardners—reinforcement (small pieces of fruit?), "moulding" the hands, and modelling. You may want to have them working in threes for this, so that they can have two "trainers". You can use this to get into a discussion about the problems of communicating without language.

It can also prove useful to give students the list of Hockett's design features of a language, and to ask them to do research on the studies of various types of animal to see how many of Hockett's features their abilities satisfy.

Set the students into groups, and ask each group to imagine that they have been given quite a large (though not infinite) research budget to devise a method of training dolphins to communicate with human beings. Also ask them to consider how will they go about the training and how they will evaluate what has been learned.

Another useful group exercise is to ask them to compare two methods of training chimpanzees to communicate with humans, discussing the advantages and disadvantages of each technique.

Having looked at numerous examples of animal cognition, you might like to set up a classroom debate on what makes human beings human, and whether we can really be distinguished from the rest of the animal world or are merely another, rather successful, example of it. Divide the class into half (trying to put people with strong views into the appropriate side), give each team 20 minutes or half an hour to research/organise their arguments, and take a class vote at the end.

Another possibility is to set up a class debate on the Terrace vs. Gardner issue. Were Washoe and the other Oklahoma chimps really using language, or was it only conditioning, as Terrace claimed?

"...MY *WHAT* IS UNDONE....?...OH! HA-HA!..SO IT IS...."

4

Student practical work

INTRODUCTION

In this chapter, we aim to provide material which will help both novice and experienced lecturers or teachers with their students' practical work. Just about every introductory psychology course involves some practical work, mainly because it is by far the best way of teaching a number of vital lessons: awareness and evaluation of methodology; practical research design, and above all, the difference between designing a study in theory, and carrying it out in practice, with real, live research participants.

Students studying introductory psychology often experience a conflict, between the very tight ethical restraints required of the modern student, and the extremely dubious practices of past psychologists which they learn about as part of their theory. However, it is possible to turn this conflict to educational advantage, by using new ethical criteria to evaluate past studies and so encouraging students to become aware of how they operate in practice. For this reason, our chapter begins with a discussion of four of the major ethical issues, and draws examples of how each of these would apply from across the syllabus.

The rest of the chapter consists of a range of new (or new-ish) ideas for practical work which can be carried out with psychology students. Some of these ideas are inevitably more complex than others, but all of them draw on theoretical issues which occur in introductory syllabuses, and involve straightforward research designs and basic-level statistical analysis. Since introductory psychology is taught in such a range of contexts, and with such a range of facilities, we also thought it better to develop practical ideas which don't require extensive equipment or facilities. Again, the ideas provided span each of the major areas of introductory psychology, and cover significant sub-divisions of each one. We hope that among the thirty practicals that we have described, every teacher will be able to find at least one or two which they could adopt, or adapt, for their own students.

PERSPECTIVES ON PSYCHOLOGY

Introduction to ethical issues

As society changes, and ethical concerns become increasingly important in all of the professions, psychologists have been re-examining their research procedures. In this section, we will be looking at some of the major ethical issues, and how they relate to existing psychological knowledge. In doing so, we will be addressing each one by drawing on examples from the main psychological topics covered by the rest of the book.

As you might expect, different areas of psychology have raised different concerns.

Covering all of the possibilities would be an unmanageable task, so in this section we have decided to focus on four key ethical issues. These are:

- **the use of deception**

- **participants being distressed**

- **animal research**

- **the application of research findings**

The examples given are not, of course, exhaustive, but they are indicative of some of the major questions in this field. In any discussion of ethical issues, though, students need to be encouraged to appreciate that there are judgements involved, rather than the rigid application of hard and fast rules. It may be unethical to deceive participants as a general rule, but there are situations where deception may be not only ethical, but even, very occasionally, morally appropriate. For this reason, it is best to treat ethical questions as topics for discussion rather than absolute rules.

Reynolds (1982) identified three criteria for ethical judgements, and in attempting to deal with debates about ethical judgements, it can help to ask your students to consider specific studies in the light of the three criteria. The three criteria are:

- **Utilitarian, cost–benefit criteria**—*do we learn more from the research than we could do from research carried out differently, and if we do, is it worth it?*

- **The effects on the participants**—*what will the outcome of our research be for the participants involved? Clearly, if covert observation has no effect whatsoever, this is different from research in which the covert intervention produces changes.*

- **Issues of individual integrity**—*have we had to engage in personal dishonesty and manipulation, and if so to what extent may this be offset by humanitarian considerations?*

These three criteria can provide a useful structure for appraisal and discussion of specific ethical debates, as well as a framework which students can use when they are attempting to revise this area.

The use of deception

Ethical concerns over deception led to the British Psychological Society stating in their 1990 guidelines that "intentional deception of the participants over the purpose and general nature of the investigation should be avoided whenever possible".

This view represented a radical change in assumptions about the nature of research, since much previous psychology was explicitly based on an assumed need to deceive research participants. The following are some examples.

Social psychology

As well as the well-known studies by Asch and Milgram, there are numerous examples of research into bystander apathy. One notable example is Latané and Darley's study in which participants sitting in a waiting room were observed while smoke poured into the room through a ventilator, to see whether the number of people present would affect how they responded.

Another example, and one which is useful for raising the issue of whether deception is inevitably a "wrong" thing to do, is Rosenthal and Jacobson's study which involved teachers being misinformed about children's intellectual abilities. This affected the children's school performance, but in the direction of the children performing better than they were otherwise likely to have done.

Cognitive psychology

Deception has often been used in this area when studying topics such as the repression of memories. Such research can involve, for instance, informing participants that their performance in a task fell below a certain standard, to see if it affects their recall. It raises questions, therefore, about the personal integrity of researchers—is it really right to sacrifice one's personal integrity in the interest of researching into a topic?—as well as the question of whether this type of approach to participants is justified and justifiable.

Biopsychology

Schachter and Singer's research on the labelling of emotions, in which participants were given false feedback about the influence of adrenalin, is one example of how deception has been used in biopsychology. Another is Ax's study which involved informing participants who were connected up to a complex-looking machine that there was a short-circuit in the apparatus, in order to study the effect of fear on physiological responses.

Individual differences

Rosenhan's initial research into professionals and students pretending to hear voices in order to gain access to mental institutions is often mentioned in this context. It's also worthwhile mentioning a follow-up study, which involved informing the staff of psychiatric hospitals that one or more pseudo-patients would try to gain admittance. Although none actually did, 41 real patients were identified by staff as likely to be pretending.

Another example is Lick's (1975) research in which phobic patients were told that they were being presented with subliminal phobic stimuli, and given false physiological feedback which implied a low level of arousal. Even though no stimuli were actually presented, this method was as effective in helping phobic patients as systematic desensitisation.

Comparative psychology

The subject matter of comparative psychology inevitably raises questions about whether you can really deceive animals. If you were really trying to push it, it could be argued that research into super-releasers and other studies of sign stimuli involve deliberate deception of the animal. You could use this to raise questions about when deception is OK and when it isn't and why it is all right to do this with animals and not humans.

You might also raise the question of "natural" deception: a hoverfly disguising itself as a wasp so as to avoid predators; a plant producing an attractive smell so as to trap insects. Dawkins and Somke and other socio-biologists argue that the very existence of communication makes deception inevitable, since it will be in some individual's interests to break the rules. Marler and others argue that this is not so, since inevitable rule-breaking would mean that animals would evolve not to take any notice of the rules at all. This type of debate, and extrapolations from it, can lead you into some very interesting discussions.

Participants being distressed or damaged

Looking at some of the earlier research in psychology it is easy to understand why those who devised the ethical principles to guide research psychologists found it important to include the principle that "the investigation should be considered from the standpoint of all participants; foreseeable threats to their psychological well-being, health, values or dignity should be eliminated." The need for this principle is evidence from the following examples.

Social psychology

Again, Milgram's research on obedience comes to mind, as does the Haney, Banks and Zimbardo role-play on prisoners and guards. You might also include Zimbardo's research into deindividuation, in which people were asked to wear coats and hoods while giving someone an electric shock, to see if anonymity increases the level of shock they give.

There is also the question of more subtle forms of distress, such as that experienced by participants in Walster's (1965) study, who were given a personality test and then deliberately given false feedback designed to lower their self-esteem. The purpose of this was to see whether they would rate a young man who has just chatted them up as more attractive as a result!

Biopsychology

Some of the early experiments in this field appear to have been hazardous in the extreme. For example, Cannon and Washburn conducted a study in which participants were instructed to swallow deflated balloons, which were then inflated to fill the stomach to investigate participants' experience of hunger.

The Minnesota Starvation Studies were another interesting set of experiments conducted in the 1930s. In these, volunteers were systematically half-starved over several weeks. Not surprisingly, as their body weight declined they became more and more obsessed with the idea of food, and more and more inclined to interpret ambiguous stimuli as having food-related content. (Content-wise, this study can be useful in discussing why Freud, working at the time that he did, considered sex to be so very important. But ethically, it seems very dubious indeed.)

Individual differences

Electric shocks were commonly used in studies in this area—not only in aversion therapy, but also in research into the differences between introverts and extroverts, to see how effectively the two groups conditioned. Studies along these lines showed that reward was better for neurotic extroverts, but punishment was more effective for neurotic introverts.

Another example would be the Valins and Ray study, in which people who were afraid of snakes were shown pictures of snakes as well as being given a "mild" electric shock when the word "shock" appeared. (They also received false physiological feedback.) In the testing

"WELL?....DO YOU FEEL HUNGRY AT ALL...?"

condition, they were asked to approach a tame 30' boa constrictor. Since they were able to approach this snake more closely than a control group, this is a useful study for asking whether the end justifies the means.

Developmental psychology

There are, of course, tremendous ethical implications in Watson's research on little Albert, in which the poor child was systematically terrified whenever he attempted to play with his white rat. If you can, it is worth getting hold of the original paper and giving it to students to read—they are often astounded by the deeply callous and manipulative attitudes of the researchers.

There are other examples of distress in developmental research, too, such as the studies of stranger anxiety which included causing short-term distress to infants. You might also consider more recent research, such as Siegal's (1990) study of Australian children which involved presenting them with a glass of milk with either a dirty comb or a dead cockroach floating on top to see if they understood the concept of contamination.

This study can be useful in helping students to distinguish between distress and damage, and mildly unpleasant feelings, such as disgust. Clearly, it is both unrealistic and undesirable to prevent research which might induce any negative emotion at all, no matter how mild—what about becoming tired after intense concentration, for instance? But at the same time, causing distress or damage has to be avoided. So at what point does one draw the line and say that a given experience is unacceptable?

Comparative psychology

This area abounds with examples of both distress and damage, such as Harlow's research on maternal deprivation in young monkeys, which showed how rhesus monkeys brought up without contact with their own kind become neurotic and emotionally disturbed. Research into stress includes Brady's work giving "executive" monkeys and others electric shock, and showing how this produced stomach ulcers. Weiss did much the same thing with rats, with similar outcomes, but this time for the control group.

Alternatively, there are Blanchard's investigations on how rats respond to the presence of cats. There are also, of course, numerous animal studies of deprivation of one kind or another, often cited in the context of nature/nurture debates. Discussing this issue will lead you straight into the next area.

Animal research

For many students, the animal research undertaken in psychology before the growth of the animal rights movements is seen as unnecessary and cruel. Students often get emotional about this issue, and it can lead you into interesting discussions about means and ends. Several examples have already been given, but some more issues come to mind.

Social psychology

Although social psychology tends to focus on human beings, earlier research often used information derived directly from animal studies, such as Calhoun's research into crowding in rats, which showed how unlimited breeding with strictly limited resources in terms of food and space produced increased stress, eventually resulting in infanticide and even cannibalism. Seligman's research into learned helplessness in dogs, induced by giving them repeated electric shocks with no means of escape, is also often perceived as one of the foundations of modern research into attributions and depression.

Cognitive psychology

Much of the research into perceptual development raises issues about the ethics of animal research, such as the many studies of animals reared under visually deprived conditions. You might also discuss Köhler's use of chimps in his studies of insight learning, which could be useful in raising the question of (a) whether animal research is inevitably a bad thing, since these animals were caged and bored, and the research at least gave them something to do; (b) the outcomes provided significant evidence for a challenge to mechanistic assumptions about the nature of learning, based on far less acceptable studies of rodents and pigeons; and (c) the basic assumption underpinning the studies was of respect for the chimpanzees' mental abilities.

Biopsychology

This area, of course, abounds with research using animals, from brain research involving ablations and lesions, to Hubel and Wiesel's use of micro-electrode recordings to study the visual cortex in live animals; from the use of castration to eliminate aggression in male rodents, to the creation of obesity in rats after lesions to the ventro-medial hypothalamus. Not forgetting, also, Lashley's studies of equipotentiality, in which progressively large proportions of the cortex were destroyed in order to investigate the effect on problem solving.

Some students may not have considered the fact that all of the animals in these experiments will have been routinely "sacrificed" in order to find out exactly where the lesion was or how the brain was affected. Steven Rose (1992) objects strongly to the use of the word "sacrificed", seeing it as disguising what is really going on. He uses the more honest term "killed" instead. You might use this to discuss the more general use of language to hide ethical concerns (such as the use of "blind" instead of "lied to", as in "single-blind", "double-blind" etc.)

Individual differences

One issue here is the way that some psychiatric treatments have been systematically derived from animal experiments, including insulin shock therapy. One of the

most important examples here is Moniz's early lobotomy on the chimpanzee Martha, which showed how this made the animal more docile and passive. From this, Moniz concluded that the frontal lobe controlled aggression and should therefore be removed in excessively aggressive people.

A more recent example of animal research in this area is the way that Gray's research into the limbic system in rodents led to the development of a new type of anti-anxiety drug. It is open to discussion whether this is regarded as a positive development or not. Gray and many other people clearly regard it as positive; animal rights campaigners and those with reservations about the medical profession do not. So this question can be a useful way of bringing the medical argument to the fore, and discussing, again, how and where we draw the line between acceptable and unacceptable research.

In a similar vein, behaviour modification and behaviour therapeutic techniques were firmly based on learning principles derived from animal research, so it is worth revisiting Pavlov's early work in this context, as well as Skinner's pigeons. Applying these approaches did help a number of people to cope better with their lives, whether the full theoretical package of behaviourism was adopted or not. So how far do the outcomes justify the studies?

Developmental psychology

One obvious area of concern here is Harlow's research into maternal deprivation, since this formed such an influential foundation for later theories of human attachment. Another connection was animal research into imprinting, since this was the direct foundation of Bowlby's ideas about the infant forming a special bond with its mother which was qualitatively unlike any other relationship—an idea which has yet to disappear, despite the lack of support, and which was the basis of the maternal deprivation debate. Students might also consider what happened to the young ducks once they had imprinted on inappropriate stimuli such as wellington boots or Lorenz.

Comparative psychology
The whole area, by definition, is about animal studies, and there are some general issues to be raised here. The most fruitful for ethical discussions often concern the nature/nurture debate, particularly when it involves raising animals in isolation, cutting off rats' tails and whiskers to prevent exploration of the environment or manipulation of objects, or even rearing pigeons in tubes to prevent practice in wing movements. You could also raise the question of selective breeding, and the use of electric shocks and brain surgery in investigations of animal behaviour.

The application of research findings
There are a number of ethical problems which can arise from the use to which research information is subsequently put. This has resulted in a growing concern about the application of research findings, and the effects of research publication. While the initial intention behind the research may be miles away from its application, the whole question of social responsibility of science means that psychologists should not be naive about how their research could be used.

The use of research also leads into questions about the ultimate purpose of psychological research. The behaviourists were in no doubt about that one: for them, the aim of psychology was to predict and control behaviour. However, more recently other values have come to the fore: prediction may be all very well, but control is a far more questionable aim. By contrast, many modern psychologists see the ultimate purpose of psychology as being to facilitate positive autonomy and self-determination in human beings and human societies.

Social psychology
At first sight, it might seem that a greater understanding of social behaviour can only be beneficial to society. It could be worthwhile getting students to consider how some of the research on persuasion, social skills training and impression management has been applied by politicians, sales personnel and others to manipulate people more effectively. The classic example of this is neurolinguistic programming in which classifications of non-verbal signals are used to assist salespeople and others to target their clientele more effectively.

You might also encourage students to consider whether having too much knowledge about the processes underpinning personal relationships actually aids or inhibits them. Students might also discuss the effect on women's self-esteem after reading numerous psychological papers involving females being rated for attractiveness; and the more general outcomes of such research in establishing scripts and inducing a generally sexist mind-set.

Cognitive psychology
One issue here is the implications of Bernstein's distinction between elaborated and restricted codes of language. Labov's critique of Bernstein established the fact that people can think just as well no matter what code of language they spoke, but the link between language and social class, particularly in Britain, and its influence on stereotyping, educational achievement, and so on, still has relevance, and can lead you into a number of discussions about the social role of different forms of language.

In memory research, knowledge about how memories become adapted and altered depending on context and personal schemata raises social questions about the reliability of eye-witness testimony, the influence of questioning of witnesses, and also the role of hypnosis in police investigations. Studies of the use of hypnosis in retrieving "lost" memories can also be mentioned, since they can easily result in the public assuming that memories are more reliable than they are. You might also get students to consider how the publication of research on false memory syndrome may affect both victims of incest and people who have been accused of incest after 20 years.

Biopsychology

A major area of concern in this topic has been theories about a possible genetic basis for negative traits such as aggression, criminality and the like. Links between genetics and behaviour can also be considered in terms of such aspects as the press furore over the search for the genetic basis of homosexuality. You might encourage students to ask why the search for such a gene is considered to be an appropriate target for research funding in the first place, as well as looking at the implications for society if anything of the kind were actually identified.

You can also draw students' attention to the use of prefrontal lobotomies and ECT in treating psychiatric patients, as well as to the search for a neurological basis of dyslexia. This in turn can lead you into discussions about labelling. Geshwind's (1984) finding that left handedness in males is linked to vulnerability, for example, could lead into discussions about how such findings might affect the employment of left-handed males.

Individual differences

To some extent, some of the problems of publication of research findings are that it may influence how people perceive themselves: to know that the Type A person is more vulnerable to stress-induced cardiac disease may worry you if you are a Type A person.

The most obvious areas of concern here revolve around race and intelligence, and the way that IQ research has been used to legitimise racist social practices. It is important that students should appreciate the socio-political role that intelligence tests have played in the past, since it is an underlying theme for a great deal of current social debate on these issues.

The idea of giving people IQ and personality tests when they apply for jobs as a means of selection should also be discussed. Are personality tests a more desirable means of selection than graphology? It is worth using this debate to familiarise students with some of the variety of different tests, including simulations and exercises, since these are commonly used in occupational selection.

In abnormal psychology, there is the use of token economies and aversion therapy as a means of controlling the behaviour of others. Ask students to consider why psychologists attempt to change people's behaviour in the first place, and whose benefit the change is for. You might also get them to consider the ethical implications of implosion therapy (flooding).

Developmental psychology

Bowlby's research on maternal deprivation is an obvious starting point, since the social implications of this particular debate are very far from over. You are likely to find that students have their own opinions as to whether mothers should or should not go out to work, and it is worth investigating just how far these are informed by scientific evidence.

There are also the social debates brought about by identifying family influences in problems such as autism and schizophrenia, or social learning influences such as the role of the media in contributing to violence in society. Society's demands for single-cause explanations has resulted in a serious distortion of the findings and led to people identifying one factor, rather than many, when explaining complex behaviour. Discussion of these issues can be structured by focusing on levels of explanation.

Comparative psychology

From comparative psychology you might raise the use of animals in advertising after being trained by operant conditioning techniques. You could also discuss the military uses of operant conditioning techniques such as the use of dolphins to carry depth charges. There is also the other side of conditioning research, such as the use of hot-housing in the United States to try to advance the young child's abilities.

The main concern over publication of research often revolves around the somewhat tenuous links between some types of animal behaviour and the way that Western human society is organised. Ideas stressing "survival of the fittest" have been proposed for denying some people health care; Lorenz's theories of aggression helped fuel Nazi ideology, and Social Darwinism also contributed to the murders committed in concentration camps.

There are numerous examples of theorists focusing on one or two species to make it appear that hierarchies, gender role differences and territorial behaviour are inevitable in human beings. Similarly, research on socio-biology has led to controversial discussions on "selfish" altruism and "looking after your own kind", and to theories emphasising only the most negative aspects of human nature. These need to be discussed in the context of bio- and behavioural diversity, and in terms of the many different levels of explanations which we can use in understanding human behaviour.

COGNITIVE PSYCHOLOGY

Sensory systems & perception

This practical allows you to explore the feature-detection theories of pattern recognition.

Method

This is a straightforward experiment, using a related-measures design.

What you will need

- Two A4 pages, each containing a 10x10 letter grid. Each grid contains 20 letter Zs, randomly placed among the other letters. The other letters in one of the grids are Ms, Ns, and Ws, distributed randomly. The letters in the other grid are Os, Cs and Qs.
- It would be helpful to have a stop-watch, but a watch with a second hand will do.

What to do

Get your students to find at least 12 participants for this study, and preferably more. The participants are then given a letter grid, and asked to cross out any Zs they can see, as quickly as possible. Time how long it takes them to do this. When they have finished, give them the other grid and repeat the procedure.

Since participants will do both grids, it is advisable to counterbalance the design, such that half of them do the "Ms" grid first, and the other half do the "Os" grid.

How to analyse the results

- Display the times taken for the two different types of grids on a chart.
- Calculate the mean time taken for each condition.
- Compare the two using a *t* test for related samples.

Discussion points

The key discussion revolves around whether it takes you longer to cross out Zs in the grid which contains letters with similar features (angles, lines, etc.) than in the one containing very different letters. Does this support feature-detection theory? Are there other possible explanations?

Students might also discuss whether the two grids were truly balanced (should the Zs appear in the same place on each grid, and how would that influence practice effects, etc.) and how well they standardised their instructions to each participant.

Attention

This practical allows you to relate self-reports of alertness to the processing of "unattended to" information, and so it can be looked at in terms of the various filter theories of attention.

Method

A laboratory-based correlation study.

What you will need

- A method of rating alertness on a linear scale. It is perfectly OK to use a simple rating scale, ranging from "very drowsy" through "same as usual" to "highly alert", and ask participants to give self-ratings.
- You will also need a paragraph containing two intermingled passages, so that one half appears in bold type or capitals and the other doesn't, for example:

"John **Sally** Major **was** was **a** facing **tall** pressure **strong** late **woman** last **with** night **fair** after **skin** he **and** announced **blue** that **eyes.** tax **She** would **had** have **always** to **been** go **seen** up. **as** The **mature** opposition **but** saw

behind this **this** as **facade** the **was** final **a** straw **very** and **different** wanted **person.** a **She** vote **knew** of **too** no **much** confidence **and** in **was** the **frightened.** government."

What to do

Get your students to ask about 15 or more participants to rate themselves on the alertness scale, and then ask them to read the passage in bold type, out loud.

Once they have finished that, the participants should then be given a piece of paper and asked to write down as many words from the non-attended passage (i.e. the one in lower-case, or ordinary type) as they can remember. The data consists of the number of words from that passage that they manage to recall.

How to analyse the results

- Display them in a table, with the number of words set against the alertness rating for each participant.
- Perform a rank-order correlation (Spearman's rho) on the two sets of scores.

"APPARENTLY, SOME PEOPLE CAN'T DO TWO THINGS AT ONCE..." "OH REALLY? THATS.....OOOF!!..."

Discussion points

The discussion might focus on whether non-attended information is processed or not, and if so, how much.

Methodological discussion might also look at some of the problems of using self-assessment and rating scales.

Memory

This practical allows you to explore whether people with developed expertise and schemas in relevant areas can recall more information than people with less developed expertise.

Method

This is a straightforward experiment, using an independent-measures design.

What you will need

- Video playback equipment.
- A videotape of a 5-minute extract from a well-known soap opera. The best ones would probably be either "Neighbours" or "Coronation Street", but you should gear it to the likely interests, or not, of the participants.
- Sheets of paper, each containing the same 20 questions about the extract.
- A list of the correct answers to these questions.

What to do

By questioning, find two groups of participants: those who are regular viewers of soap operas, and those who don't watch them. These may be among your own students, or they may prefer to go and find others.

Firstly, show the participants the 5-minute video recording. Then give them the questions to complete.

Questions can be marked by reading out the answers and asking them to mark their own or each other's, but make sure that you collect the sheets in afterwards and that there are no changes to the scores.

How to analyse the results

- Display them on a chart, comparing "Soap addicts" and "Naïve viewers" on the number of questions they answered correctly.
- Calculate the median answer for each group, and compare them.
- Perform a Mann–Whitney U test to compare the two samples.

Discussion points

The key question focuses on whether fans (i.e. those with highly developed concepts/schemas about these programmes) have a greater ability to recall information than non-fans.

As well as raising ideas about schemas, and even about memory processing (does interest affect recall?), it can also allow for some interesting discussions about experts and novices.

Methodological discussion points might centre on the "either/or" nature of the fans/non-fans distinction.

Language comprehension & production

This study allows you to explore the differences between the spoken word and written language.

Method

A case study approach, using qualitative analysis.

What you will need

- A portable tape recorder.
- Pen and paper.

What to do

The task is to explain to a visiting Martian how to use a supermarket. Get each of your students to ask one other person to do this, firstly by interviewing them and tape-recording what they say, and then by asking them to write down their explanation.

Once they have collected this data, they will need to transcribe the verbal report on the tape, so that it can be compared with the written one.

Each student can look in detail at just one person's accounts; or, if you prefer, they can group their answers together.

How to analyse the results
- Since they will be using qualitative analysis, this needs to be structured very clearly. They might compare the two reports on the following characteristics:
  (a) the length of both explanations: is the spoken or the written account more lengthy?
  (b) If there are differences in length, why? What sort of detail or additional information is included in one account but not the other?
  (c) Does one account use more pronouns while the other uses the relevant nouns? Since pronouns may imply an assumed shared knowledge, what does this tell us about the difference between spoken and written language?

Discussion points
The points given above, of course, are also for discussion, since in qualitative analysis there is no simplistic distinction between the analysis and the theoretical discussion.

In addition, you may like to discuss the use of qualitative analysis at all: how necessary it is, and how it can be done systematically without losing meaning.

Thinking
This practical explores some of the difficulties we face when we try to solve problems, and how we often put limits on ourselves as a result of our previous experiences.

Method
This is a straightforward experiment, using an independent-measures design.

What you will need
- About 40 sheets of paper, each containing nine dots arranged in a square (make sure there are wide margins around it, see below).
- Pens or pencils.

PROBLEM

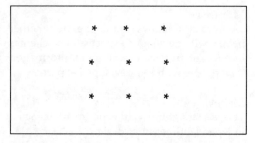

What to do
Ask your students to find at least 20 or so participants. They will be asked to solve the classic nine-dot problem, so make sure they haven't done this problem beforehand.

Each participant is given one of the sheets of paper, and asked to: "Connect these nine dots with four straight lines, without taking the pen off the paper or going over the same line twice." Half of the participants should just be given the problem as it stands. The other half should be given an additional instruction: "You don't have to keep your pen within the limits of the square if you don't want to." Each participant should be given three minutes in which to complete the problem.

SOLUTION

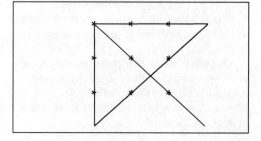

How to analyse the results
- Display the data on a two-by-two frequency table, with "full instructions" and "limited instructions" as the two columns, and "solved" or "not solved" as the two rows.
- Compare the results of the two groups using a chi-square test.

Discussion points
The discussion is likely to focus on factors which inhibit problem solving, and in particular on the way that we tend to assume that problems have boundaries, with very little evidence. This may be related to other limiting factors in human problem solving. It can also be related to research into the use of cues to guide thinking.

Methodological discussion might look at problems of subject variability: are some people just naturally better at solving puzzles than others?

SOCIAL PSYCHOLOGY

Conversation & communication
This study allows you to see whether political allegiance influences the type of explanations people give to explain poverty.

Method
An observational study using both qualitative and inferential analysis.

What you will need
- Pen and paper.
- Research participants who are willing to state their political preference, e.g. strong supporters of either the Conservative, Labour, or Liberal Democrat parties.

What to do
You will need to find approximately equal numbers of supporters from each party. Fifteen of each would be about right, although you could just about manage with ten.

Ask the research participants to write down five reasons which they think explain why some people are poorer than others.

If you want to structure this, you could give each participant a sheet of paper which had "Some people are poorer than others because..." followed by a blank space for them to write on, repeated five times. But just writing the straight answers down would be OK.

Analysing the results
- The responses which people give can be classified in terms of whether they are focusing on dispositional or situational causes.
- A two-by-two table can be drawn up to display the results, showing the number of dispositional and situational factors each party's group chose.
- If you want to use inferential statistics, a chi-square test applied to the two-by-two table would be appropriate.

Discussion points
Firstly you can see whether there is any association between the types of explanations given and the political allegiance of participants. If a difference does emerge you could try to explain why this would be. Schema and script theory can be useful here.

You might also want to examine why some people are reticent about telling you who they vote for. Problems of deciding whether reasons are dispositional or situational can also be explored. Would it have been preferable to have given the research participants prearranged information which could be easily classified, instead of an open-ended approach?

Are there other coding dimensions which might have been useful, other than situational and dispositional attributions?

Interacting with others

This study explores the effect of leadership styles on members of a group.

Method

An experimental study using qualitative analysis.

What you will need

- Two students who are willing to adopt different leadership styles, e.g. democratic and authoritarian.
- A suitable group task, e.g. to design a group project to study person perception, or to build a four-foot high tower using newspapers and sellotape.
- 10–16 research participants, sorted into two groups. It is best to use psychology students for this.

What to do

Make sure that the two students acting as leaders are well briefed, privately, on their roles, and that other research participants know that they are the leaders.

Explain the task to them, and ask them to complete it within a set time, such as 15 minutes.

When the time is up, ask each research participant to write down what factors they felt helped with the task, and what inhibited it. You might also ask them to express whether they enjoyed working with the group, and whether they felt able to express their ideas.

Analysing the results

- The starting point is to see whether both groups finished the task, and if so how long it took them.
- Similarities and differences between the groups could then be examined in terms of the factors which helped or hindered them.

Discussion points

Initially, you can focus on whether there was any difference in the performance of the two groups.

It is also essential to look at the nature of the interaction between the leader and the members of the group. Did the group accept the authority of the leader? How easy was it for the leader to maintain their style?

The qualitative analysis would probably consist of "key" quotes from people, describing their experiences of being in the group. You might also look at any attributions which were given as to why the group succeeded or failed in the task.

It would also be useful to discuss the ethical question of whether the research participants were being deceived or not, particularly if they are psychology students.

Person perception, attraction, & relationships

This study allows you to explore whether self-efficacy beliefs affect the person's willingness to keep on trying to complete a task.

Method

An experiment using an independent-measures design as well as inferential statistics.

What you will need

- Three tennis balls.
- A stop-watch, or watch with a second hand.
- Possibly a tape recorder, but this is not essential.
- Two groups of research participants, one consisting of "sporty" people and the other consisting of people uninterested in sport. About 15 people in each group, or more.

What to do

Inform the participants that you are interested in the problems faced by people performing new tasks.

Tell them that their task is to juggle the three balls, and keep them up in the air for about two minutes. (If you like, you can get one of the popular "Teach yourself juggling" books to explain the technique).

Let them know that they are free to give up whenever they like, and time how long they take before they either complete the task, or give up. (It is a good idea to put a time limit on their attempts.)

If the participants are willing, you could tape their comments as they try this new task.

Analysing the results
- Draw up a table which compares the times taken by the "sporty" people before they gave up, and the time taken by the non-sporty types.
- Analyse the results using an independent-measures *t* test.

Discussion points
Initially you can see whether people who are good at sport spend longer trying to master a new skill. Do non-sporty types give up quickly because they believe that they are no good at things like that?

If you have tape-recorded comments, look for ones which indicate underlying self-efficacy beliefs. Are there differences between the two groups? Are there variations within the "sporty" groups, depending on which sport they play?

Was timing people before they gave up an adequate measure, or were there better ways of collecting suitable data for this?

Attitudes
This study lets you consider some of the strategies used in advertising.

Method
An observational study using content analysis.

What you will need
- Pen and paper.
- A video tape and video recorder.

- Tape recordings of about five advertisements. (It might be helpful if they are all advertising similar products, e.g. chocolate bars, soap powder, beer, or cereals.)
- Research participants (normally a class of psychology students).

What to do
Ask the students to devise a chart to help them to analyse the advertisements they are about to see. This chart would contain a number of categories focusing on aspects of persuasion, such as the source of the message (e.g. expert, "ordinary person" etc.), the tone of the message (e.g. informative, friendly, emotive), the type of music used, whether voice-overs were used, symbolism and imagery, etc.

Then show the participants the advertisements, and ask them to analyse each one using the chart.

Analysing the results
- Draw up a set of tables showing the categories used, and how each advert measured up on each category.
- In some cases, you may find it appropriate to use a chi-square test.

Discussion points
The first thing is to look at the tables to see if they indicate any striking regularities (do soap powder adverts always use "ordinary people", did all the adverts feature "happy" music, were voice-overs always male, etc.).

Then identify differences between the adverts. How were advertisers trying to differentiate their products from others of their type? What about the background setting of the advertisement? Both similarities and differences can be discussed in terms of what they tell us about the strategies which advertisers are using to persuade people to buy the product. So can other questions, such as the context in which the adverts were shown.

Methodological discussion points are likely to focus on problems with this type of analysis. Were the categories appropriate? Were all the advertisements coded in a similar way? Were there significant features of the advertisements which could not be recorded owing to the lack of suitable categories?

Conflict & co-operation

This study allows you to explore the notion that crowds inevitably turn into mobs.

Method
Developing a psychometric scale. An experimental study using inferential statistics.

What you will need
- Pen and paper.
- Five slips of paper, each naming one of the following: (1) shopping crowds, (2) pop concert crowds, (3) sporting event crowds, and (4) major public event crowds, such as Royal Weddings or V.E. day (you might want to leave this one out if your students have no experience of them), and (5) rioting crowds.
- Facilities for typing up a list and duplicating it.
- A group of psychology students.
- A set of research participants, who might just as well be other students attending the college.

What to do
Set your psychology students into five groups and ask each group to develop a list of 10 adjectives which describe their personal experience of being in the type of crowd described on their slip of paper. (If they have never been in a rioting crowd, you could let them look in textbooks or use their imaginations for the adjectives for this one.) If you have time, you could swap the slips around, so that each group has an opportunity to describe each type of crowd.

Collect together all the adjectives from all the groups (some will overlap) to draw up a final list.

Ask the students, working individually or in groups, to assign each adjective a numerical value between 1 and 10, where 1 would be the most unpleasant experience, and 10 would be the nicest one. Calculate an average score for each adjective. Then randomise the list of adjectives, and print it onto slips of paper. Have these duplicated for the experiment.

Use only the first three types of crowd on the list (shopping, pop concert and sports), unless there happens to have been a major public event lately and lots of people went to it. Ask research participants to describe their personal experience of being in one of these types of crowd by ticking 10 adjectives on the slip which best describe their experience. Remember to emphasise that it is their own real personal experience which counts.

Collect at least 15 responses for each type of crowd. Whether you use an independent or repeated-measures design depends entirely on whether you have research participants with experience of all three types of crowd.

Analysing the results
- Calculate the numerical score for each response, and draw up a table showing the mean score and standard deviation for each type of crowd.
- Then take the crowds in pairs (shopping/pop concert) and compare the two.
- Use a Mann–Whitney U test if it is independent-measures, or a Wilcoxon Sign test if it is repeated-measures.

Discussion points
Developing the psychometric test allows you to raise questions of reliability, validity and standardisation: Is this a reliable measure? How might you find out? Is it a valid measure? Are there dimensions of the crowd experience which are not covered? How would you feel if you were always alone and never part of a crowd at all?

Contrasting the adjectives describing the "real-life" crowds and the other one could be interesting. Were they the same? If not, why not? What can this tell us about media representation of personal experience?

In the experiment, comparison of scores for different types of crowd allows you to raise similar questions. Do these correspond with crowd experience as presented by the media and most psychology textbooks?

DEVELOPMENTAL PSYCHOLOGY

Infancy
This study allows you to explore some of the nuances of parents' perceptions of infants.

Method
A qualitative study using the semantic differential.

What you will need
- Sheets of paper containing semantic differentials with seven dimensions, as follows:

good	....	bad
clean	....	dirty
cold	....	hot
tense	....	relaxed
active	....	passive
rough	....	smooth
weak	....	strong

- Four clear acetate (OHP) sheets and pens.
- Four groups of parents:
  (a) mothers of young children (under 5s),
  (b) mothers of older children (over 7s),
  (c) fathers of young children,
  (d) fathers of older children.

What to do
Ask each of your students to find two, three or four parents (depending on the size of the class) and to ask them to complete the semantic differential for the word "baby".

Analysing the results
- First, calculate the median score on each of the dimensions, obtained for each group of participants.
- Draw the semantic differential of the median score for each group on an acetate sheet, and overlay them.
- Note any points of difference between the groups.

Discussion points
In practical terms, it is interesting to ask whether any prospective research participants found themselves unable to do the semantic differential.

It may be interesting to look for consensus around the term "baby".

Grouping the data also allows students to look at individual differences. What was the range of scores in each group?

You could look at whether parents of older children (whose experience with babies is further in the past) show more negative associations than others. This, if it is the case, can be linked with cognitive dissonance theory.

You can also explore gender differences: were there systematic differences between the associations made by mothers and those made by fathers?

Early childhood
This study allows you to explore intellectual and visual realism in children's art.

Method
This is an experiment, using an independent-measures design.

What you will need
- A cup with a decoration on it (e.g. a flower design) and a handle.
- Drawing paper and pencils.
- Two groups of children:
  (a) a group aged 6–7,
  (b) a group aged 8–9.

- Permission to run the study from those responsible for the children concerned.

What to do

Place the cup in front of the children so that the handle is not actually visible, but the floral design is.

Ask the children to draw the cup, as they see it. (It is better to ask each child individually, to avoid peer group influence.)

Collect the drawings and record whether the children included the handle that was not in view.

Analysing the results

- Draw up a 2 x 2 table, showing how many from each group included the cup handle, and how many left it out.
- If you have at least five in each cell of the table, you could test for significant differences using a chi-square test.

Discussion points

Initially students can consider whether there is a difference between the age groups. Do the drawings focus on what the children actually see or what they know? The findings can be used to discuss the idea that young children draw what they know is there, rather than what they see (intellectual realism) whereas older children draw what they can see (visual realism).

This may lead into discussions about socialisation, and how far Western children are taught to see only visual realism as "correct".

This study also raises questions about children's understanding of the task, and students might like to consider how different types of phrasing of the instructions may influence the child's understanding of the task.

Middle childhood

This study allows you to compare different phases of moral development in childhood.

Method

Experiment using an independent measures design and a Mann–Whitney U test.

What you will need

- A short story detailing the activities of two children. Jo breaks a glass deliberately by disobeying an instruction, whilst Sam breaks eight glasses accidentally.
- Pen and paper.
- Two groups of children, ideally 15 or so in each group:
  (a) a group aged between 6 and 9,
  (b) a group aged between 11 and 14.
- Permission to run the study from those responsible for the children concerned.

What to do

Read the story to each child individually.

Afterwards, ask the child whether Jo or Sam was the naughtier, and why. Write down their answers.

Then ask them to give a score out of 10, expressing just how naughty each child was.

It might also be interesting to ask the children whether they would punish Jo or Sam, and if so, the punishment they would give.

Analysing the results

- Draw up a 2 x 2 table comparing the two groups, and whether "Jo" or "Sam" was seen as naughtier.
- Compare the scores obtained from the two groups using a Mann–Whitney U test.
- Use the child's opinions about punishment as qualitative data to enhance the analysis.

Discussion points

Firstly, ask whether younger children focus on the amount of damage done rather than the intention underlying the behaviour. Also, look at the punishments and reasons given by the children. These ideas can be related to both Piaget's and Kohlberg's theories of moral development.

The problems of using stories to discuss moral reasoning can also be explored along with discussions of whether such stories aid our understanding of moral development.

In practical terms, students may like to explore the question of whether their research participants fully understood the concept of a 10-point rating scale.

Adolescence

This study is designed to see whether adolescents believe that they have differing experiences of life-events from older people.

Method

A correlation study, using Spearman's rho.

What you will need

- Sheets of paper listing 15 life-events taken from the Holmes and Rahe scale, for example, marriage, parenthood, divorce, moving house, unemployment, Christmas, bereavement, etc.
- Pens.
- Adolescents as research participants.

What to do

Ask each participant to rate the life-events on the list on a scale of 1–10, with 1 being least stressful and 10 the most. They should do this twice: once for themselves, and once for their closest parent.

Calculate the total scores given to each life-event in each of the two categories.

Analysing the results

- Draw up a table of the total scores given to each life-event for each group.
- Draw a bar-chart, with pairs of bars for each life-event, to illustrate the results. Alternatively, draw up a scattergram.
- Perform a correlation (Spearman's rho) between the pairs of scores obtained for each item in the whole set of life-events.

Discussion points

The first question is whether both groups rate the life-events in similar ways, which can be identified from the table.

The outcome of the Spearman's rho can be discussed to see whether there is a positive relationship between these perceptions: Do both groups rate "moving house" as the least stressful, and "death" as the most, for example?

This study also allows students to explore the problems involved in assigning marks to stressful life-events, and may lead into other issues, such as whether life-events occur "on time" or not.

The age range of the groups might also be explored as a confounding variable, since adulthood covers a wider age span than adolescence.

Development in adulthood
This study is designed to look at images of the elderly in British society.

Method
An observational study using content analysis.

What you will need
- A supply of newspapers, preferably local ones.
- Pens and paper.

What to do
Ask your students to go through the newspapers, collecting stories featuring people over 65.

Develop a set of coding categories for the stories, such as: victim/victor, powerful/powerless, rich/poor, helpless/in control, active/inactive, etc.

Code each story's content using these categories.

Also note visual images, e.g. physical settings, facial expressions, etc.

Analysing the results
- Draw up a table showing the number of items fitting into each content category for each story.
- You can convert this data into percentages of the themes apparent in the whole story.

- Calculate the mean number of category items for the stories as a whole.

Discussion points
This study is likely to raise discussion about the practical problems of classifying news stories and the difficulties of categorising behaviour.

The research also allows students to consider how the elderly are represented. Terms like "frail", "helpless" and "victim" can be considered in terms of their contribution to older people's self-esteem.

It might be possible to use a semantic differential to analyse some of these key words.

INDIVIDUAL DIFFERENCES

Intelligence
This practical allows you to explore Howard Gardner's idea of "interpersonal intelligence" as one of seven separate types of intelligence.

Method
Experimental study using inferential statistics and qualitative analysis.

What you will need
- Two photographs of genuine couples (i.e. people who are in a relationship) and two photographs of people who are just pretending to be a couple. Note: make sure the people in the photographs have given their consent.
- Scoring sheets, which provide boxes for indicating whether each of the four couples is genuine or false, and space for writing a reason by each choice.
- Pens.

What to do
Ask the students to select about 30–40 participants, half of whom are studying psychology, and half of whom are studying physics, maths, chemistry, or engineering.

Each participant is shown the four photographs and asked to identify which pair they consider to be a genuine couple, and which they do not, and to write down reasons for their answers.

Analysing the results
- Draw up a 2 x 2 table of "psychology" and "non-psychology" students as the rows, and "accurate" and "inaccurate" as the columns.
- Perform a chi-square test on the result.
- Undertake a qualitative analysis of the reasons given on the answer sheets, looking particularly at the factors used to decide whether the couples were genuine or not.

Discussion points
This study should allow you to discuss some of the difficulties in assessing interpersonal intelligence, as well as whether an interest in psychology really affects your ability to judge other people. By using psychology and non-psychology students you can discuss the role of interest in intelligence, and perhaps also experience in looking at/writing about interpersonal issues.

Depending on the outcome, you might explore which non-verbal cues people use to select genuine couples, e.g. angle of the bodies, leaning towards each other, cues of relaxation, socio-economic match, similarity, physical contact. Should sensitivity to non-verbal cues be linked to intellectual skills; or is it, as Gardner suggested, an entirely different skill?

Personality: Factor theories
This practical allows you to explore the problems involved in assessing one's own personality, and the extent to which our perception of ourselves matches other people's assessment of us.

Method
A correlational study using Speaman's rho.

What you will need
- About 20 copies of a list of traits as would be used in a typical personality questionnaire, such as Cattell's 16PF (e.g. emotional, outgoing, assertive, conscientious, shy, practical, suspicious, self assured, relaxed).
- A set of score sheets which contain a 7 point scale for each of the personality traits, rating the applicability of the traits, from 1 = "doesn't describe me/them at all" to 7 = "describes me/them perfectly".

What to do
Choose about 20 participants who enjoy assessing themselves and hearing other's assessments of them. (Please don't attempt this project with people who are very sensitive to other's opinions of them!)

Ask the participants to rate themselves on each of the traits.

Then ask each participant to give a copy of the score sheet and the list of traits to a close friend, and to ask the friend to rate the participant.

Analysing the results
- Calculate the discrepancy between the two ratings for each pair of people, and then find the average discrepancy for the whole group. Do this separately for each trait on the list.
- Draw up a bar-chart showing the average discrepancy between the participant and friend's ratings on all of the traits together. The bars will fall either above or below a central line: bars above should show where the participant rated themselves more highly on the trait than the friend did; bars below should show where the participant rated themselves lower than the friend did.
- Perform a Spearman's rho correlation test on the data, to see how strong the relationship is between the two measures.

Discussion points

Using a friend's assessment raises the whole notion of objectivity: is it likely that the friend was truthful in their assessment? Would it have been better if the friend knew that the target person could not find out about the rating they were given? Or would this then raise ethical questions about deception? This can lead into issues of social desirability and response bias.

The adequacy of trait rating scales as measures of personality can also be raised. Would it have been better if people identified their own traits, rather than adopting established ones?

In general, the practical raises questions about the extent to which our opinion of ourselves correlates with how other people see us. This can lead to a discussion of phenomenological vs. behaviourist approaches: who is the most appropriate person to assess personality traits, the insider or the outsider?

Cognitive approaches to personality

This practical allows you to explore Kelly's personal construct theory, in terms of whether adolescents and adults share similar constructs.

Method

Case studies involving repertory grid techniques and some qualitative analysis.

What you will need

- A set of role-based personal construct elicitation forms, which contain space for a list of six significant other people, and spaces to say how any two of them can be considered similar, and different from a third (e.g. "Janet and Michael are impatient, but Sally is calm"). The significant others suggested should fit with established social roles, such as mother, father, brother, sister, partner, best friend, teacher, etc.

- A set of repertory grids: blank tables with space for eight constructs at the top, and six elements down the side.

What to do

Ask the students to select two groups of research participants, one of adolescents (16–19), the other of older people (30–50). Ideally, you want at least 12 in each group, but each student could ask just one or two other people.

Give each participant a construct elicitation form to complete. Then proceed to the analysis.

Analysing the results

- The first part of the analysis involves devising the repertory grid itself, and this has to be done in consultation with the research participant.

- Then, enter the constructs which they produced in the first stage as the columns on a repertory grid, and list their elements (significant other people) as the rows. Ask the participant to enter ticks or zeros depending on whether the construct applies to each of the other people on their list or not.

- Taking the group of research participants as a whole, collect the words used to describe the constructs, and list them in two columns: "adolescents" and "adults".

- Perform a qualitative comparison of the different types of words used by the groups.

Discussion points

On a practical level, consider the construction of the repertory grid. Did the research participants have problems verbalising their constructs, or did they find it relatively easy?

The study demonstrates the idiographic nature of repertory grids, and so raises the question of whether a method designed to look at individual cognitions can really be used to compare people with one another.

You might also consider how far personal constructs are individual, or whether they are influenced by cultural factors. Was there a tendency for adolescents to use certain constructs more than others? If so, this raises the whole question of social representations, and whether personal construct techniques allow us to take wider social factors into account.

Were there systematic differences between the two groups, or were the differences between individuals more important, regardless of their age? This leads into a discussion of between-group and within-group variance.

You might also look at problems of cross-sectional studies of ageing, as opposed to longitudinal ones.

Approaches to abnormality

This practical allows students to investigate everyday use of terms relating to mental illness or disturbance.

Method

An observational study involving content analysis.

What you will need

- A week's set of newspapers, preferably the tabloids.
- Pen and paper.

What to do

First, ask your students to develop a list of words which are commonly used by the newspapers to describe abnormality ("crazy", "neurotic", "lunatic", "nutter", etc.).

Then ask them to go through the newspapers, underlining each of those words as they appear, and listing who is being described in these terms (e.g. terrorists, football hooligans, politicians etc.).

Also, ask them to collect any alternative words which didn't appear on the list.

Analysing the results

- Organise the data into three columns: the words used, who it was describing, the context in which it was used. Identify major themes in the third column: political activity, sport, national interest, etc.
- Count the number of times each of the themes appeared during the week. See whether different words or types of words are associated with different themes.

Discussion points

The prime discussion point here is how far words are used to influence public perceptions. Are words relating to abnormality systematically used to discredit those with a particular political viewpoint? Is this different from the way that they are used when describing sport? And how far does this support the ideas of Laing or Szasz about the social role of mental illness?

You could also relate the use of these words to the seven features of abnormality identified by Rosenhan and Seligman, to see how far they connect with more serious perceptions of mental disturbance (if they do).

Finally, there is the question of the role of the media in influencing our ideas about mental illness, and the social stigma attached to the label.

Forms of psychopathology

This practical allows you to investigate general knowledge about common psychiatric disorders, and to see whether psychology students are better informed.

Method

An independent-measures experiment involving inferential statistics.

You will need

- Lists, each describing 24 different psychiatric symptoms expressed in everyday language (e.g. "sometimes becomes unable to move" instead of "catatonic fugue"). The symptoms should be drawn equally from the three diagnostic categories of schizophrenia, bipolar depression and personality disorder, arranged in random order, and numbered from 1–24.

- Score sheets, which give the three diagnostic categories and space for the respondent to enter the number of each symptom which applied to that category.

What to do
First, test your group of students, asking them to list the symptoms which apply to the categories. Keep their score sheets separate, although individuals need not be identified.

Then, ask each student to go and test one other person, who is not studying psychology, nursing, or other related subjects.

Ask them to match the sample as far as possible—i.e., to find someone similar in age and background to themselves.

Then calculate the number of correct answers made by each respondent, according to the score sheet. Again, individuals need not be identified, although the groups must be kept separate.

Analysing the results
- Calculate the mean score for each group and present it in a simple table.
- Perform an independent-measures *t* test on the scores to see if there were significant differences between the two.

Discussion points
The first question is whether there were common areas of misconception which appeared in the results. Did people construe schizophrenia as "split personality", for instance?

You might consider how the rating scale could be improved, or whether a better list of symptoms could be constructed. Also, whether the data was really equal-interval, as the use of the *t* test implies.

The study also raises the more general question of how mental illness is understood in society, and whether people actually do understand what is involved. Do social stereotypes and stigmas act to prevent us from developing a full understanding of the problems involved?

Therapeutic approaches
This practical allows you to examine some of the factors that contribute to people's fears.

Method
A correlational study.

What you will need
- A scoring sheet, which lists characteristics of animals along with a 7-point rating scale for each one. The characteristics should include speed of movement, attractiveness, size, and fearsomeness (i.e. whether the respondent is likely to be frightened of them or not), but you could also include some "distracters", such as furriness, brightness of colouring, etc.
- A list of four animals that people are likely to be frightened of. The most common are probably cats, spiders, wasps, cattle, dogs, and snakes.

What to do
Ask each of a group of respondents (who might easily be your class of psychology students) to complete four score sheets: one for each of the four animals on the list.

Collect the results as paired scores for correlation.

Analysing the results
- Draw up a scattergram, pairing "fearsomeness" and "attractiveness". Then do the same, comparing "fearsomeness" with each of the other variables (these can be distributed between students, to share the workload).

- Perform Spearman's rho correlation tests to compare the different sets of data.

Discussion points

In practical terms, you might discuss what these results tell us about factors contributing to people's fears. Were there other characteristics which might have been included? Are there better ways of measuring how much someone is likely to be frightened by a particular animal?

In general terms, you might discuss why some animals are more likely to be feared than others. This can lead on to an investigation of some of the reasons for people's fears, and the possible influence of early experience and/or modelling.

Discuss of personal experience can lead to discussions of the role of learning in fear as well as introducing the distinction between fears and phobias.

BIOPSYCHOLOGY

Drugs & the nervous system

This study allows you to investigate the different ways that people perceive everyday drugs.

Method

A psychometric study using some qualitative analysis.

What you will need

- Pens or pencils.
- Duplicated sheets containing a set of semantic differential charts. Each sheet should contain six semantic differentials, headed "milk", "tea", "coffee", "beer", "wine", "whisky". The semantic differential is a set of 7-point scales, representing 10 different dimensions. There are a number of possibilities, but a good set to use is the following:

angular	....	rounded
weak	....	strong
rough	....	smooth
active	....	passive
small	....	large
cold	......	hot
good	....	bad
tense	....	relaxed
wet	....	dry
fresh	....	stale

These dimensions should be arranged as a vertical set, so that the rating scales are exactly in line with each other.

What to do

Ask research participants to mark an appropriate point on each dimension of the semantic differential, for each of the drinks. You may need to explain that they should use their imaginations, and describe the overall impression that the drink gives them, rather than producing a factual description.

Draw up a profile for each drink, by drawing a line which zigzags down the rating scales joining up the points which have been marked.

How to analyse the results

- Calculate the mean score obtained for each dimension, with respect to each drink. Use this score to draw up a set of "general" semantic differential charts representing each drink.
- Use a qualitative analysis to highlight systematic differences in perceptions of the different drinks involved.

Discussion points

It may be useful to begin by discussing the perceptions of the various drinks involved in terms of particular drugs: milk (naturally occurring morphines), tea (tannin, weak caffeine), coffee (strong caffeine), different types of alcoholic beverages. Does the image which the drinks seem to have reflect the potency of the drug? Would it have been useful to have some general categories too, such as "caffeine" and "alcohol"?

The way that the semantic differential can identify subtleties and nuances of perception is a good topic for discussion. Students may like to extend this study by exploring the potential of this method for investigating other topics, e.g. attitudes towards illegal drugs among their peers and other groups; descriptions of different social groups, etc.

Hemisphere function
This study is designed to investigate whether either right- or left-handed people are likely to be better mathematicians.

Method
Experiment using an independent-measures design.

What you will need
- Two groups of research participants, such that group A consists of left-handed participants and group B consists of right-handed ones.
- A set of arithmetic problems.
- Pens and paper.

What to do
Perform a pilot study to see how long it takes participants to complete the questions. In the main study, reduce the time allowed, so that they will not be able to finish the task.

Give each participant the question sheet and ask them to complete as many of the questions as they can, in the time limit available.

How to analyse the results
- Calculate the mean and the standard deviation for each group, and display these in a table, comparing right-handers and left-handers according to the total number of questions answered correctly, the mean, and the standard deviation.
- If you like, you can perform a Mann–Whitney *U* test for independent samples on the data.

Discussion points
The initial discussion will need to centre on ideas about cerebral dominance, and whether right-handers (left-hemisphere dominant) may be better at mathematics than left-handers (right-hemisphere dominant).

Some consideration should also be given to how right and left-handedness were selected in the first place, as well as whether a test for a right hemisphere function, such as spatial or artistic skills, should have been included. The discussion should also explore alternative explanations for ability or competence at arithmetic.

Stress, anxiety & emotion
This study allows you to examine whether there may be a relationship between daily hassles and everyday illness.

Method
An observational study using correlational analysis.

What you will need
- Pens and paper.
- Duplicating facilities.

What to do
The first part involves devising a questionnaire with two scales: one about everyday hassles (money worries, noise, interruptions etc.), and one about minor illnesses (headaches, colds, flu, stomach ache etc.). Spend some time constructing and piloting the questionnaire, ensuring that there are an equal number of questions for each scale, and that they are evenly distributed. Then duplicate the questionnaire, and distribute it to at least 20 participants.

How to analyse the results
- Draw up a scattergram, which plots each person's "hassles" score against their "illness" score.

WITH MOUNTING APPREHENSION, TREVOR BEGAN TO SUSPECT THAT THE
REMOTE CONTROL HAD ONCE MORE BEEN PLACED OUT OF ARM'S REACH.

- Use a Spearman's rho to investigate whether there is a significant relationship between the two variables.

Discussion points

Initial discussion is likely to centre on the adequacy of the questionnaire. Should it have included a scale for positive experiences as well as negative ones? How could it have been improved? Were some "hassles" experienced by almost everyone, while others were less common?

If a positive correlation has been obtained, discussion might focus on possible explanations for this, bearing in mind that correlation does not infer causality. The theoretical implications of a lack of correlation are also interesting: do illness and stress only correlate for major life-events and not for minor ones? If so, why?

Motivation

This practical explores the influence of external cues in food intake.

Method

Experiment using an independent-measures design.

What you will need

- Two video tapes, one containing a series of 10 adverts for food, and one containing a series of 10 adverts for different products, e.g. washing powders. (Avoid those with presenters who also advertise food).

- Sheets of paper each containing 10 7-point rating scales, from 1 = "never" to 7 = "as soon as possible".
- Pens or pencils.
- Video replay equipment.
- Several bowls containing Smarties.

What to do

Conduct the study after lunch, in the hope that the participants will not be too hungry.

Inform each participant that they are being asked to rate a set of advertisements in terms of how likely it is that they would buy the product. Provide them with rating scales and pens for that purpose.

Place a bowl containing a known number of Smarties on the table by each participant, saying that they can help themselves if they want to, as a way of thanking them for taking part.

Count the number of Smarties left in each bowl when the video tape is finished, and debrief the participants.

How to analyse the results

- Draw up a table, with the experimental condition (food/non-food adverts) as the columns, and the total and mean amounts of Smarties consumed as the rows.
- If you like, you can use an independent-measures *t* test to analyse the data.

Discussion points

Problems with the experimental design and ways that it could be improved will be one focus for discussion.

The deception and subsequent debriefing of participants also raises ethical questions which should be discussed. Individual differences in taste and food intake may also be a factor.

The main discussion, though, is likely to centre around the role of external cues in food consumptions, and the influence of consumerism on our behaviour.

Sensory information processing

This study allows you to investigate whether people's cognitive perceptions of smells link with their supposed function in aromatherapy.

Method

An observational study, using descriptive statistics.

What you will need

- Samples of five essential oils: peppermint, geranium, lavender, eucalyptus, and clove.
- Some paper tissues.
- Sheets containing a checklist of five minor ailments, repeated five times. The five minor ailments are: stomach upsets, mild depression, headache, colds and toothache.
- Pens or pencils.

What to do

Cover the labels of the oils, and label them A, B, C, D, E, randomly instead.

Put a drop of oil A onto a tissue, and ask the research participant to smell it.

When they have done so, they should mark on their checklist for oil A which ailment they think it is supposed to help. Repeat the process for the other oils.

You may also like to ask them to name the oil, if they can, just for interest—but not until after they have marked their checklist.

How to analyse the results

- Draw up a bar-chart for each oil, by adding up the number of answers given in each category.
- Compare the bar-charts, to see whether the functions of some oils were more readily identifiable than others.

Discussion points

Obviously, the study has many weaknesses, and these need to be explored. The first thing is probably to discuss the effects of familiarity. Some of the oils (e.g. eucalyptus) are likely to have been recognised instantly, while others may be less familiar. How did this influence the results?

There are also questions such as whether more variables should have been included—more ailments, or a larger number of oils. Then there are wider questions, such as whether it is reasonable to expect to identify therapeutic virtue from smelling something; whether the nature of olfactory pathways in the brain may explain the effectiveness of aromatherapy, etc.

COMPARATIVE PSYCHOLOGY

The basis of behaviour

This study is designed to investigate some of the problems of observing animal behaviour, including anthropomorphism, inter-observer reliability, and questions of scale.

Method

An experimental study, involving content analysis and chi-square test. The independent variable is the individual difference between the two observers.

What you will need

- A pet animal: mammal or bird (goldfish are not suitable).
- A timer or watch.
- Pens and paper.

What to do

The observers will need to work in pairs, and each pair needs to observe an active pet animal for a period of 10 minutes. During that time, each person should write down what the animal does. The records need to be independent, with both observers watching the animal at the same time, but not knowing what each has written down. The observa- tions should be carried out before any discussion of how it will be analysed takes place, so that the observations are uninfluenced. Once the observation is finished, the two reports are compared and analysed.

The first content analysis involves two categories, and is concerned with the scale of the observation:

a) Molar behaviour, i.e. actions involving movement of the whole body (e.g. "dog turns round").

b) Molecular behaviour, i.e. actions which involve only a part of the body (e.g. "dog wags tail").

The second content analysis involves three categories, and is concerned with degrees of inference or interpretation:

a) Strictly behavioural descriptions (e.g. "hamster stands on hind legs in corner of box and moves body upwards").

b) Functional descriptions of behaviour (e.g. "hamster climbs up side of box").

c) Anthropomorphic inferences (e.g. "hamster tries to escape from box").

How to analyse the results

- Firstly, read through the reports to see whether the observers did actually record the same behaviour from the animal, or whether some people noticed some actions while their partner didn't. Count the number of times that the reports fail to coincide in the actual events that they report.
- Secondly, perform two content analyses by counting the number of times that different types of observation have been recorded.
- Once each content analysis has been performed, present the outcomes in a table, with the two observers as the two rows, and the categories as the columns.
- Perform a chi-square test on the outcome of the second content analysis.

Discussion points
This practical raises all sorts of questions about conducting observational studies. Students might like to discuss inter-observer reliability, the degree of inference which people habitually make when studying animal behaviour, unconscious anthropomorphism, and the judgements observers invariably make about what "size" of behaviour is actually worth recording ("hamster twitches whisker"?).

In particular, the study helps to make students aware of the sheer difficulty of noting animal behaviour without interpreting it, and how powerful our human tendency to interpret what we see can be. This can lead to discussions about techniques for overcoming such problems, such as time-sampling or categorised observations, and their costs and benefits.

Reproductive behaviour
This study is designed to build on the previous one, by comparing two different approaches to structured observation.

Method
An observational study, involving time sampling and behaviour charts, and using descriptive statistics.

What you will need
- Pen and paper.
- A timer or stop-watch.
- The opportunity to observe maternal or attachment behaviour in some animals. This might be a sheep and lambs in a field, a park with ducks and ducklings in springtime, or a cat with active kittens. (See note, below.)

What to do
Firstly, get the class to devise a behavioural sampling sheet, listing behaviours which they expect to observe (feeding, calling, grooming,

following, etc.). Make sure that it has a column for "other". Also draw up time-sampling sheets, with space for times in the margin, but no other structure.

Divide the students into two groups, and ask them to observe the animals for a continuous 10-minute period. One of the groups will use behavioural sampling, and make ticks whenever they see behaviour which fits into the categories on the sheet. The other group will use time sampling. Every 40 seconds, in response to a signal, they will note down what they see going on.

Ask the students how useful they thought the method was as they were doing it.

How to analyse the results
- Collect the behavioural category data, and draw up a bar-chart showing the frequency of each type of behaviour during the observational period.
- Use the time-sampling data to develop a list of the kinds of behaviour which were observed, and the number of times each came up.
- Draw up a bar-chart showing the frequency of each type of behaviour during the observational period.
- If there are relatively few animals involved, use the time-sampling data to draw up "profiles" focusing on the actions of individual animals during the observational period.

Discussion points
The discussion is likely to focus on the advantages and disadvantages of the two techniques: behavioural sampling may record more instances, time-sampling may mean that crucial actions are missed, etc. The need to pilot the behavioural category chart is also likely to feature in the discussion. Students should be encouraged to discuss these in terms of considerations like inter-observer reliability, ecological validity, and the difficulties of unstructured observation.

Other questions of interest are: which behaviours occurred most and least frequently; how this concurs with maternal/attachment behaviour as portrayed in the textbooks; and whether there were any observations which were unexpected or surprising.

Note: Real-life observation is by far the best for this study. If that's totally impossible, you could try to make your own video of a field of sheep or some kittens, although make sure that you stand the camera on a tripod if you do. Wildlife videos are not usually very good, as the cameraman determines what you observe, although they are a lot better than some home-made videos. So if all else fails, you could fall back on something like "Meerkats United", but make sure you play it without the sound on.

Social organisation

This practical allows you to explore personal space among human beings. It is suitable for students who take a regular train journey lasting for half a dozen stations, or a moderate length bus journey.

Method
Observational study using qualitative analysis.

What you will need
- A pre-drawn plan of the seats in the carriage.
- A set of transparent overlays (overhead projector acetate sheets).
- A pen which will write on the transparencies.

What to do
First, invite the class to predict where people are likely to sit, through discussion of "personal space" and other theories.

When the observer gets on the train or bus, they should position themselves with a clear

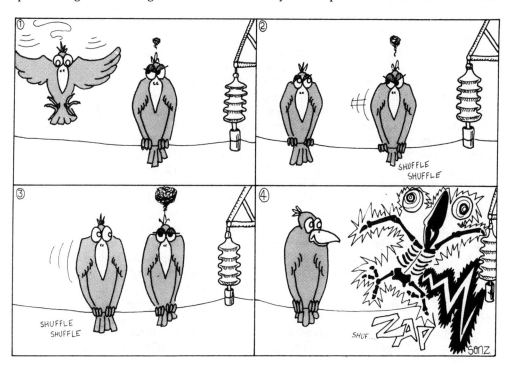

but unobtrusive vantage point (e.g. at the back of the bus). Begin by plotting the position of each person on the first transparency sheet, laid over the plan of the carriage. They may also use a code to plot the position of bags etc. on seats. At each station, or significant bus stop, the observer places a new transparency over the previous ones, marks where new passengers have chosen to sit, and indicates those who have left.

How to analyse the results
- The results can be displayed as a sequence of diagrams, indicating each new picture as each transparency is overlaid on the others.

Discussion points
Initially, students should look at how people space themselves out and whether any rules seem to be operating. For example, do people always choose an empty double seat rather than sitting next to someone else? Do people prefer to sit next to doors? What strategies do people use to prevent others from sitting next to them?

At a slightly higher level of discussion, students may discuss theories of personal space and territoriality, including the idea that territoriality is simply an evolutionary extension of personal space; different types of personal space and temporary territory; boundary conflicts and so on. They can compare their observations with the class predictions.

While this study does fall within ethically acceptable bounds, since the people being observed are in public anyway and may therefore reasonably expect their behaviour to be under public scrutiny, students may also like to explore some of the ethical issues concerned with covert observation.

Communication & information
This is a study designed to investigate human use of non-visual sensory cues. It explores whether those who believe they have a good sense of direction are more sensitive to non-visual signals than those who do not.

Method
Experiment, using an independent-measures *t* test.

What you will need
- A blindfold.
- A playing field or park with open space.
- A sports tape-measure, for measuring 10 metre distances, etc.
- Ten space markers (handkerchiefs, scarves, etc.).

What to do
First, ask the participants to assess how accurate they think their sense of direction is, on a scale of 1–10. Use their self-rating to divide them into two groups, one of people who think they have a "good" sense of direction and the other of people who think they have a "bad" one.

Then go out to the playing field or park, and mark out a circle with a 10m radius. Place one marker at the centre point, and eight of the others around the circle, so that in the end, the circle is 20m across, and marked off at 45 degree angles. Decide on one of the edge markers as the "home" base, and make sure everyone including the current participant knows which one it is.

Take the first research participant into the centre of the circle, and then blindfold them. Spin them round a few times. When they have stopped, give them one minute (timed) to orient themselves, on the basis of the sensory cues around them. When they are told that the minute is up, they should set off to walk to the "home" base, stopping when they believe they have reached it.

Use the tenth marker to indicate where they have stopped.

Take two measurements to indicate accuracy (or otherwise): the degree of deviation from the target (remember that the markers are set out in 45 degree intervals); and the distance, measured in terms of how far they are from the centre when they stop.

Ask the participants how they knew, or judged, which way to go.

How to analyse the results
- Draw up a table comparing the two groups, using degree of deviation and distance as the two columns, and the groups as the two rows.
- Conduct two independent-measures *t* tests comparing the two groups, one on each of the measurements obtained.

Discussion points
The main focus of the discussion will be on the types of sensory information which people reported using, and on their ability to function without their primary sense of vision. There may also be a question of unconscious cueing from the experimenters, or from traffic noise, etc.

The outcome of the *t* tests is likely to lead into discussions about the whole idea of the sense of direction: whether human beings do have one, whether it gets overlaid by modern living, whether it involves un-consciously receiving sensory messages and so on.

There is also the question whether self-perception is an accurate way of assessing sense of direction: were there people in the "bad" sense of direction group who actually performed well?

Animal cognition
This is a study designed to investigate people's perceptions of their pets' behaviour.

Method
An interview study involving thematic qualitative analysis.

What you will need
- An interview schedule.
- Ideally, small hand-held tape recorders, but failing that, pen and paper.

What to do
First, work out the interview schedule. The purpose of the interview is to get people to talk about their pets' intelligence. Questions such as "what is the most intelligent thing you have seen your pet do?" are therefore appropriate. Ensure that the schedule is loose, and encourages people to talk freely.

Researchers should work in pairs, with each pair interviewing either two or four pet owners. You should advise the researchers to keep the interviews relatively brief if they can—about 10 minutes should be sufficient. If they wish to keep the conversation going longer, they should stop recording after 10 minutes.

The general findings will be collated together according to a set of agreed themes. These themes should be discussed by the whole group after the interviews have been conducted, but before the pairs of researchers have analysed their individual results. The themes might be categories such as "obtaining food", "seeming to understand speech", "feigning illness", etc.

How to analyse the results
- Each pair of researchers should look through their notes (or listen to their tapes), and identify how the types of behaviour which they have been told about will fit into the main themes.
- They should also identify significant quotes, which will illustrate how the interviewee interpreted the event. In the report, they should use these quotes as the "data" in their discussion of the different types of intelligence apparently shown by pet animals.

Discussion points

This study raises a number of issues, including questions of richness in qualitative analysis and questions about the reliability and validity of account-based information.

The type of information obtained from the study can be discussed in terms of the range of behaviours shown by pets, their adaptability to demands of owners, questions of individual "character", etc. It is also interesting to relate the question of pet intelligence to studies of the effects of enriched environments on animal brain development.

Given the difference between pet lives and those of laboratory animals, and the suggestion that the enriched environment provides a qualitatively different type of experience, students may also be encouraged to speculate about how a systematic study of pet intelligence might be conducted, and what such a study would involve.

Students might also consider to what extent the types of animal "intelligence" identified in this study link with the types of animal cognition studied by comparative researchers.

5

Essay questions

INTRODUCTION

In this chapter, we have provided a full set of essay questions, covering all the different aspects of introductory psychology discussed in this book. These questions can be used in many ways: as class assignments or homework; as timed essays providing practice for examinations; as the basis for training in essay planning; and as self-assessment essays for students to use when revising.

There are many different types of essay question included here, giving a range of different types of essay-writing experience: some are largely empirical, requiring students to look at and evaluate research evidence; others are applied, requiring students to appraise psychological knowledge in the light of its usefulness for everyday living; while others border on the philosophical, requiring students to take a higher-order perspective over the knowledge which they have been acquiring.

PERSPECTIVES ON PSYCHOLOGY

General perspectives

- "Despite claiming to be a science, psychology is actually no more than common sense." Use psychological evidence to argue against this view.
- "The problematic relationship between the mind and the body still plagues psychology." Discuss.
- What particular problems would psychologists face in explaining behaviour if they fully endorsed the view that humans have free will?

Current approaches & historical roots

- Evaluate the contribution of *either* psychoanalysis *or* behaviourism to psychology.
- Psychology is not a unified science, but "a collection of more or less loosely affiliated disciplines, each with its own peculiar concepts and laws, its own methods and techniques" (Beloff). Discuss.
- "The study of animals may be interesting in its own right but does not help us to understand human beings." Discuss.

Major issues in psychology

- "The idiographic approach offers a great deal to our understanding of human beings." Evaluate this point of view, using specific examples.

- Can a truly reductionist approach ever help us to understand human psychology?
- "To ask whether human behaviour is due to our nature or our nurture is illogical." Discuss.

Motivation & emotion

- Discuss some of the physiological and psychological factors that could contribute to someone saying, when offered more food, that they couldn't eat another thing.
- "Psychological research into both motivation and emotion has been seriously distorted by reductionist assumptions." Discuss.
- Compare and contrast any *two* theories of emotion.

Research methods

- Is it true that experiments only give us information about how strangers interact in the highly artificial and unusual social setting of the psychological experiment?
- Discuss the role of single case studies in aiding our understanding of human behaviour.
- Critically discuss the use of scientific method in psychology.

The conduct of research

- What particular factors should psychologists consider before they attempt to control or change someone's behaviour?
- Using examples, discuss the ethical problems involved in conducting psychological research.
- "Despite their claims of being scientific, psychologists who use observations to further their research are merely voyeurs invading other people's privacy." To what extent do you support this view?

COGNITIVE PSYCHOLOGY

What is cognitive psychology?

- What are the main issues involved in looking at cognitive psychology as a perspective?
- Discuss the methods of study used in cognitive psychology.
- What use is cognitive psychology for people in the real world?

Sensory systems & perception

- How does the way that visual information is processed in the brain affect our perception?
- Do we have to learn how to see?
- Compare and contrast a top-down and a bottom-up theory of perception.

Attention

- Describe and discuss some theories of selective attention.
- What do we know about divided attention?
- What factors have been found to influence vigilance?

Memory

- Compare and contrast Atkinson and Shiffrin's theory of memory with the levels of processing approach.
- Why do we forget?

- How have the findings from memory research been applied in everyday life?

Language comprehension & production

- What are the main processes involved in reading?
- How is it that we understand spoken language?
- Discuss the relationship between language and thinking.

Thinking

- Compare and contrast problem solving in human beings and computers.
- How do people form concepts?
- What factors need to be considered when we are looking at how people make decisions?

SOCIAL PSYCHOLOGY

The contexts of social interaction

- What particular problems arise when trying to study social behaviour within the traditional experimental approach?
- Discuss some of the factors that contribute to the self-concept.
- Are we merely the sum of the social roles that we play?

Conversation & communication

- Discuss the role of non-verbal communication in social interaction.
- To what extent do attribution theories aid our understanding of our own and other people's behaviour?

- Discuss some of the reasons we might misjudge people.

Interacting with others

- Using psychological research, discuss some of the reasons why people do what they say they don't want to do.
- "Some are born great, some achieve greatness and some have greatness thrust upon them." Discuss this view of the emergence of leaders in the light of psychological research.
- Discuss some of the advantages and disadvantages of working in groups.

Person perception, attraction & relationships

- Why are we more likely to be attracted to some people rather than others?
- Describe and evaluate the attempts of psychologists to explain the formation and breakdown of relationships.
- "Social exchange theory takes the magic out of romance." Discuss.

Attitudes

- Using psychological research, discuss some of the problems involved in relating people's attitudes to their behaviour.
- What psychological advice would you give to an advertiser who wanted to promote a campaign to get people to give up smoking?
- Critically evaluate some of the methods used to measure attitudes.

Conflict & co-operation

- Discuss some of the problems of reducing sexism or racism in society.

- What psychological evidence is there to suggest that aggression is *not* a basic instinct?
- What factors can influence our willingness to help other people?

DEVELOPMENTAL PSYCHOLOGY

History & methods of developmental psychology

- Discuss some of the philosophical perspectives which have influenced developmental psychology.
- How have *either* Bowlby *or* Piaget contributed to our understanding of child development?
- What particular difficulties arise for psychologists when attempting to conduct research on child development?

Infancy

- Is the infant's world really a "blooming, buzzing confusion"? Illustrate your answer with psychological evidence.
- How far can a child's development be advanced through enrichment?
- Discuss the formation of attachments in early childhood. To what extent does psychological research suggest that disruption of such attachments affects the future development of the child?

Early childhood

- Can linguistic development be advanced by environmental influences?
- "Play is merely an excess of energy. It has no function." Discuss.
- How far does psychological research suggest that a child's thinking is entirely different from that of an adult's?

Middle childhood

- Discuss some of the weaknesses of stage theories of moral development.
- How does a child learn to read?
- Give evidence for and against the idea that schooling aids the child's intellectual development.

Adolescence

- Is adolescence inevitably a time of "storm and stress"?
- Discuss some of the social and cultural factors which contribute to adolescent development.
- In what respects and to what extent does the adolescent's thought differ from the child's?

Development in adulthood

- "Marriage is psychologically healthy for men, but psychologically unhealthy for women." Discuss.
- How can psychological knowledge be helpful in ameliorating the harmful effects of unemployment?
- Discuss some of the positive aspects of ageing.

INDIVIDUAL DIFFERENCES

General issues

- What do we mean by the term individual differences?
- Discuss some of the significant dimensions along which people are commonly compared.
- Are human beings born, or are they made?

Intelligence & intelligence testing

- "Intelligence is an outmoded concept." Discuss.
- Critically evaluate methods used to assess whether intelligence is determined by genetic or environmental factors.
- To what extent can psychologists be said to be able to measure intelligence?

Personality: Factor theories

- Drawing on research evidence, discuss some of the problems which psychologists face when trying to assess personality.
- "We are merely the sum of the roles we play." To what extent would personality theorists argue against this view?
- Critically evaluate type and trait approaches to personality.

Cognitive approaches to personality

- Compare and contrast one cognitive theory of personality with one different personality theory.
- Using examples, discuss how the cognitive approach to personality can be used to help people overcome problems.
- "Changing how people think doesn't necessarily change how they behave." Discuss.

Approaches to abnormality

- "Normality is the absence of abnormality." Discuss.
- Critically evaluate the medical model of abnormality.
- Why is diagnosing someone as "mentally ill" a controversial act?

Forms of pathology

- What are the advantages and disadvantages of being able to classify mental illness?
- What particular difficulties arise in making diagnoses of childhood disorders?
- How may genetic, neurochemical and environmental factors contribute to our understanding of mental disorders such as schizophrenia?

Therapeutic approaches

- Discuss some of the therapeutic approaches which may help in the treatment of people suffering from phobias.
- Compare and contrast the psychoanalytic approach to the treatment of abnormal behaviour with one other approach.
- What problems arise in assessing whether a particular treatment of mental disorders is effective?

BIOPSYCHOLOGY

What is biopsychology?

- How may the study of physiological structures and systems enhance our knowledge of human psychology?
- What is meant by the term reductionism? What particular difficulties arise in using physiological reductionism to explain human behaviour?
- "Animal rights are unimportant when human illnesses are at stake." Discuss the arguments for and against this idea.

The nervous system

- How have case studies contributed to our understanding of the human nervous system?

- Discuss the action of psychoactive drugs on the central nervous system. How may these effects influence human behaviour?
- How can an evolutionary perspective help us to make sense of the structure of the central nervous system?

Language, hemisphere function & memory

- Critically evaluate some of the techniques used to identify localised functions within the brain.
- How far does it make sense to argue that the right and left hemispheres of the brain have different functions?
- How have animal studies contributed to our understanding of the physiological basis of learning and memory?

Stress, anxiety & emotion

- Outline and discuss some of the main physiological mechanisms involved in anxiety stress.
- What have psychologists discovered about the reasons why people respond to stress in different ways?
- Compare physiological explanations of emotion with other explanations.

Sleep, arousal & motivation

- Why do we sleep? Discuss how physiological and psychological insights may help to answer this question.
- To what extent can animal studies help us to understand eating disorders in human beings?
- Discuss the advantages and limitations of a knowledge of physiological mechanisms in understanding human motivation.

Sensory information processing

- "Pain perception is entirely a matter of mental control." How far does the evidence from physiological psychology support or challenge this statement?
- Compare and contrast how we process visual and auditory information.
- What can the study of neural pathways in the visual system tell us about how we perceive visual information?

COMPARATIVE PSYCHOLOGY

Comparative psychology & evolution

- Discuss some of the advantages and limitations of applying findings from animal research to human beings.
- Descartes believed that humans and animals are entirely different from one another. Do you agree? Give reasons for your answer.
- The behaviour of animals is often studied in the laboratory rather than in the natural environment. What are the advantages and disadvantages of these two approaches?

The basis of behaviour

- Discuss the problems in trying to assess the relative importance of genetic and environmental factors in the determination of behaviour.
- Critically evaluate Lorenz's hydraulic model of inherited behaviour.
- "Even classical and operant conditioning depend on cognitive processes." To what extent do you agree with this statement?

Courtship, mating & reproduction

- Outline and discuss some of the theories which have been put forward to explain animal courtship.
- To what extent can studies of parental behaviour in animals throw light on human parental behaviour?
- Discuss what we know about imprinting in terms of Tinbergen's four areas of comparative psychology: development, mechanisms, function, and evolution.

Social organisation

- What do you understand by the term territoriality? Discuss the explanations which have been put forward to explain different aspects of animal territoriality.
- Are dominance hierarchies inevitable in animal social organisation? Give evidence for your answer.
- Outline and discuss peace-making strategies shown by primates.

Communication & information

- How can Tinbergen's four areas of comparative psychology help us to understand birdsong?
- Describe and discuss some studies which illustrate the problems involved in studying cetacean communication.
- What do we know about chimpanzees' natural forms of communication, and how have researchers studied it?

Animal cognition

- Can animals think? Give evidence for your answer.
- Discuss the view that human beings are the only creatures capable of using language.
- To what extent do you agree with the idea that learning is a genetic process? Give evidence for your answer.

6

Topics for revision

INTRODUCTION

This chapter consists of material which can be used to help structure revision exercises. There are many ways to revise a topic, of course, and a number of the exercises suggested in Chapter 3 (Class or seminar activities) are suitable for that purpose. But it is often helpful to have some material which will provide a focus for the revision, and this is what we have tried to provide here.

The chapter is divided into sections following the main areas of psychology; and within that the areas are subdivided into topics. For each topic, we have provided a set of key words or phrases and the names of some influential figures (usually psychologists, but sometimes significant philosophers or other scientists). One productive way of using these, therefore, is to ask students to provide definitions for the key words, and accounts of the work of the key figures.

There are also five revision questions provided for each of the topics. These questions have been carefully designed so that they do not overlap with the essay questions found in Chapter 5, but complement them instead. Students can use them as self-assessment questions when they are revising for examinations. Alternatively, they can be used as formal exercise questions, or to

provide a focus for group research or class discussion. There are over two hundred of these questions in the chapter, which we hope will provide plenty of scope for any of these applications.

PERSPECTIVES ON PSYCHOLOGY

General perspectives

Key terms
introspection, associationism, psychophysiological parallelism, nature/nurture controversy.

Significant figures
Aristotle, Descartes, Darwin

Revision questions
- What is the iceberg model of the mind?
- Give three arguments challenging the view that psychology is just common sense.
- Can any of Plato's ideas be considered relevant for modern psychology?
- What is psychological parallelism?
- Briefly outline the principles of associationism.

Current approaches & historical roots

Key terms
psychoanalysis, behaviourism, behaviour therapy, psychometrics, sociobiology, humanistic psychology

Significant psychologists
Freud, Watson, Piaget, Maslow

Revision questions
- Outline the methods used by psycho-analysts to study the unconscious mind.
- Briefly describe the fundamental assumptions of the behaviourist approach to psychology.
- Distinguish between "European" and "American" social psychology.
- What are the advantages and disadvantages for psychologists of studying animals in the natural environment?
- What are the principles of client-centred therapy?

Major issues in psychology

Key terms
reductionism, determinism, idiographic, nomothetic, cognitive neuropsychology

Significant psychologists
James, Allport, Nisbett and Wilson

Revision questions
- Define reductionism, and give three criticisms of a reductionist approach to psychology.
- What is determinism?
- Outline the four levels of environmental influence described by Lerner.

- What are the shortcomings of a nomothetic approach to understanding human beings?
- Briefly describe the main types of research carried out into con-sciousness.

Motivation & emotion

Key terms
motivation, homoeostasis, drive-reduction theory, James–Lange theory, Cannon–Bard theory, cognitive labelling

Significant psychologists
McDougall, Hull, Schachter and Singer

Revision questions
- What are the main problems encountered by attempting to explain motivation in terms of instincts?
- How has the concept of homoeostasis been used to explain motivation?
- What are the main components of emotion?
- Briefly describe one study which supports the James–Lange theory of emotion.
- What is the cognitive labelling approach to emotion?

Research methods

Key terms
empiricism, law of parsimony, operational definition, self-actualisation, demand characteristics, correlational designs, single-case studies, self-report data

Significant figures
Popper, Rogers, Silverman

Revision questions
- Briefly outline the hypothetico-deductive approach to scientific enquiry.
- What are the main types of variables involved in the experimental method?
- Describe what is meant by demand characteristics, and discuss their implications for psychological research.
- Describe two advantages and two disadvantages of the single case study as a research technique.
- What are the major disadvantages of using questionnaires to study human behaviour?

The conduct of research

Key terms
ethical principles, informed consent, deception, animal experiments, preparedness, equipotentiality, reinforcement, social control

Significant psychologists
Milgram, Skinner, Seligman

Revision questions
- Explain the concept of a power deficiency with respect to psychological research participants.
- Briefly outline some of the alternatives to using deception in psychological research.
- List the 10 ethical principles for psychological research published by the British Psychological Society in 1990.
- Give two arguments for and two against the use of animals in psychological research.
- What ethical concerns are raised by the practice of behaviour modification?

COGNITIVE PSYCHOLOGY

What is cognitive psychology?

Key terms
top-down, bottom-up, serial processing, parallel processing, cognition, computer metaphor

Significant psychologists
Boden, Neisser, Weiskrantz

Revision questions
- Distinguish between top-down and bottom-up theories.
- What is parallel processing?
- Outline briefly what is meant by the computer metaphor.
- Explain how the study of brain damage may help us to understand cognition.
- What does the term information processing mean?

Sensory systems & perception

Key terms
sensation, perception, perceptual organisation, pattern recognition, constructive theorists, computational theory of perception

Significant psychologists
Gregory, Gibson, Marr

Revision questions
- How does visual information reach the brain?
- Describe two studies which imply that perception is learned, and two which imply that it is innate.

- Describe the Gestalt principles of perception.
- List the main points of Gibson's theory of direct perception.
- What are the main stages in how we develop a recognisable image of an object, according to Marr?

Attention

Key terms
selective attention, capacity theory, divided attention, bottleneck models of attention, vigilance, automatic processes

Significant psychologists
Treisman, Broadbent, Moray

Revision questions
- Give two everyday examples of selective attention.
- What are the distinguishing features of focused auditory attention?
- How does task difficulty affect divided attention?
- Describe an example of automatic processing.
- What factors influence effective vigilance?

Memory

Key terms
multi-store theories, levels of processing, semantic and episodic memory, encoding specificity, amnesia, mnemonics

Significant psychologists
Atkinson and Shiffrin, Craik and Lockhart, Tulving

Revision questions
- What are the three main differences between short-term and long-term memory?

- Distinguish between episodic and semantic memory.
- How does levels of processing theory challenge the two-process model?
- What is a schema?
- List the major reasons which have been suggested for why we forget.

Language comprehension & production

Key terms
eye movements, linguistic competence, schemata, plans, verbal thought, lip-reading

Significant psychologists
Bransford and Johnson, Van Dijk, Vygotsky

Revision questions
- What are the basic physical processes involved in reading?
- How do we come to identify and perceive speech?
- How does context affect our understanding of language?
- Outline three differences between speech and writing.
- List the three major theories concerning the relationship between language and thinking.

Thinking

Key terms
mental set, computer simulation, artificial intelligence, heuristics, concept-formation, representativeness and availability

Significant psychologists
Wason, Rosch, Kahnemann, Tversky

Revision questions
- Describe a study of mental set.

- What are the main differences between novices and experts?
- Describe the levels of concepts identified by Rosch, and give three related examples, illustrating each one.
- Describe one example of computer simulation or artificial intelligence.
- List the main heuristics involved in decision making and judgement.

SOCIAL PSYCHOLOGY

The contexts of social interaction

Key terms
social role, social schema, script, social identification, self-fulfilling prophecy, ethnocentricity, self-concept, account analysis, action research.

Significant psychologists
Schank and Abelson, Tajfel, Harré

Revision questions
- Outline the four main types of social schema.
- What are the basic motives which lead to social identification?
- Describe Rosenthal's study of the self-fulfilling prophecy.
- What is new paradigm research?
- What is ethnocentricity, and how can it be related to psychological theories of the self?

Conversation & communication

Key terms
non-verbal communication, discourse analysis, attributions, social representations, lay epistemology

Significant psychologists
Argyle, Heider, Moscovici

Revision questions
- List the main types of non-verbal cues.
- Outline three common strategies identified in Van Dijk's study of racist discourse.
- What are the four main dimensions which Lalljee identified as necessary for understanding explanations?
- Distinguish between the correspondent inference and covariance theories of attribution.
- Describe a study of social representations.

Interacting with others

Key terms
audience effects, social loafing, bystander intervention, conformity, obedience, group polarisation, leadership.

Significant psychologists
Latané, Asch, Milgram

Revision questions
- Define the following terms: coaction, social facilitation, social loafing.
- Briefly outline social impact theory.
- Distinguish between compliance, internalisation and identification.
- What explanation did Milgram propose for why people would act against their consciences when ordered to do so?
- Describe the conditions under which groupthink will occur.

Person perception, attraction, & relationships

Key terms
self-efficacy beliefs, primacy effects, implicit personality theory, social exchange theory, matching hypothesis, cognitive similarity

Significant psychologists
Bem, Bandura, Walster, Duck

Revision questions
- Define the following terms: implicit personality theory, primacy effects, personal constructs.
- Describe a study illustrating the importance of self-efficacy beliefs.
- What are the main factors that psychologists have identified in interpersonal attraction?
- Briefly describe the main non-verbal indicators of attraction.
- Outline the eight dimensions for studying relationships described by Hinde.

Attitudes

Key terms
value and attitudes, cognitive, conative and affective dimensions, cognitive dissonance, Likert scale, semantic differential

Significant psychologists
Fishbein, Festinger, Hovland

Revision questions
- Outline the three main functions of an attitude.
- Who developed the theory of reasoned action, and what does it state?
- Explain why cognitive dissonance can be a factor in producing attitude change.
- Distinguish between source, message, and receiver variables in persuasion.
- Compare three different ways of measuring attitudes, giving the advantages and disadvantages of each one.

Conflict & co-operation

Key terms
aggression, prejudice, the authoritarian personality, collective behaviour, mob psychology, altruism

Significant psychologists
Lorenz, Bandura, Le Bon

Revision questions
- Outline the frustration–aggression hypothesis.
- Contrast two different theories of prejudice.
- What are the main requirements for reducing prejudice?
- Describe and evaluate a study of deindividuation.
- What factors have been shown to be effective in maintaining orderly crowd behaviour?

DEVELOPMENTAL PSYCHOLOGY

History & methods of developmental psychology

Key terms
schema, assimilation, accommodation, maturation, evolution, attachment, ontogeny, phylogeny

Significant figures
Darwin, Binet, Bowlby

Revision questions
- Outline two environmental factors which may inhibit development.
- Briefly compare the developmental theories outlined by Watson and Gesell.
- What did Piaget mean by the epigenetic landscape?

- Briefly outline the basic principles of Vygotsky's approach to child development.
- Discuss some of the problems presented by stage theories of development.

Infancy

Key terms
foetus, texture gradient, constancy, sensori-motor, strange situation

Significant psychologists
Gibson, Piaget, Bower

Revision questions
- Briefly outline the evidence for the idea that psychological development may be occurring in the pre-natal period.
- What are the main sensory capacities of the neonate?
- Give two ideas for and two ideas against the view that motor development is purely a function of maturation.
- What methods have psychologists used to investigate infant perception?
- Describe one study of smiling in infants.

Early childhood

Key terms
signifier, symbol, visual realism, autism, conservation, egocentricity, animism, zone of proximal development

Significant psychologists
Vygotsky, Garvey, Donaldson

Revision questions
- What steps are involved in the young child's acquisition of a vocabulary?
- What are the main types of play which have been studied by psychologists?

- How do children's drawings change as the child becomes older?
- What did Piaget mean by egocentricity, and how did this affect cognitive development?
- Describe one study which challenged the Piagetian view of cognitive development.

Middle childhood

Key terms
concrete operations, transitive inference, orthography, IQ, idiot savant, moral development

Significant psychologists
Dunn, Harris, Bryant, Kohlberg

Revision questions
- According to Piaget, what cognitive abilities does the child acquire in middle childhood?
- Give two examples of cross-cultural evidence, one which challenges Piaget's theory of cognitive development, and one which supports it.
- How may family members influence the child's social development?
- What are the main stages involved in learning to read English?
- Briefly outline psychological research on the child's acquisition of numeracy.

Adolescence

Key terms
formal operations, social role, psychosocial stages, context specificity, transsexual, hypothetico-deductive reasoning, gender identity

Significant psychologists
Erikson, Mead, Coleman

Revision questions

- What are the major psychological approaches to gender identity in adolescence?
- Outline the distinctive features of Freud's view of adolescence.
- Contrast Piaget's and Keating's views of adolescent thinking.
- In what way may adolescent thinking differ from adult thought?
- Why did Erikson identify role transition as most important during adolescence?

Development in adulthood

Key terms
gerontology, ageism, stereotype, lifespan development, life course, life-event, bereavement, selective optimisation

Significant psychologists
Rutter, Levinson, Baltes

Revision questions
- List and briefly describe Erikson's psycho-social stages of development.
- What are the fundamental principles of the lifespan approach to development?
- What are the six key elements in parenting identified by Rutter and Rutter in 1992?
- Describe one psychological investigation of marriage.
- What is meant by the term "selective optimisation", and how has it been applied to understanding older people?

INDIVIDUAL DIFFERENCES

Intelligence & intelligence testing

Key terms
intelligence, IQ, intelligence testing, reliability, validity, twin studies, triarchic intelligence, multiple intelligence

Significant psychologists
Binet, Galton, Sternberg, Gardner

Revision questions
- How can reliability and validity be measured?
- Describe one advantage and one weakness of using twin studies to investigate the nature–nurture debate on intelligence.
- Briefly describe what is meant by factor theories of intelligence.
- What criticisms have been made concerning the use of IQ tests as evidence in the nature–nurture debate on intelligence?
- Outline the three subtheories of intelligence which make up Sternberg's triarchic model.

Personality: Factor theories

Key terms
traits, types, personality test, 16PF, EPQ, test–retest reliability, projective tests, extroversion, situationism, interactionism

Significant psychologists
Cattell, Eysenck, Mischel

Revision questions
- Describe one specific type theory of personality, and discuss some of its weaknesses.
- What is meant by the term "personality trait"?
- What are some of the problems encountered when assessing personality using questionnaires?
- What are the principles underlying the thematic apperception test?
- What are the "five robust features" of personality described by McCrae and Costa?

Cognitive approaches to personality

Key terms
phenomenology, personal constructs, repertory grid, client-centred therapy, social cognition, self-efficacy

Significant psychologists
Bandura, Kelly, Rogers

Revision questions
- What are personal constructs?
- How is a repertory grid constructed, and what can it be used for?
- According to Rogers, what are the fundamental psychological needs of human beings?
- What characteristics are required in those who practise client-centred therapy?
- Outline what is meant by self-efficacy beliefs, and describe one way in which the concept has been applied by psychologists.

Approaches to abnormality

Key terms
normal, abnormality, medical model, DSM-III-R, psychosocial stressors, aetiology, diasthesis

Significant psychologists
Kraepelin, Szasz, Rosenhan

Revision questions
- Give one advantage and one disadvantage to using a "features" approach to define abnormality.
- What is meant by the social deviance approach to abnormality?
- Outline and evaluate Rosenhan's study of psychiatric diagnosis.
- What are the five axes of DSM-III-R?
- Briefly describe the diasthesis–stress approach to mental disorder.

Forms of psychopathology

Key terms
schizophrenia, unipolar depression, bipolar depression, phobias, anxiety disorders, obsessive-compulsive disorders

Significant psychologists
Laing, Beck, Brown and Harris

Revision questions
- What problems are associated with attempting to diagnose schizophrenia?
- Briefly outline the symptoms associated with bipolar depression.
- Why is the idea of a "personality disorder" controversial?

- What is an obsessive-compulsive disorder, and how have clinicians attempted to deal with it?
- Evaluate whether the concept of "disruptive behaviour disorder" simply medicalises a social problem.

Therapeutic approaches

Key terms
behaviour therapy, systematic desensitisation, aversion therapy, reinforcement, biofeedback, psychoanalysis, cognitive therapy, rational-emotive therapy, ECT

Significant psychologists
Wolpe, Freud, Bandura, Ellis

Revision questions
- Describe two different approaches to helping people with phobias.
- Briefly outline two forms of therapy based on operant conditioning.
- What are the main techniques used in psychoanalysis?
- Describe the significant features of Aaron Beck's cognitive therapy for depression.
- Briefly outline the basic principles of rational-emotive therapy.

BIOPSYCHOLOGY
What is biopsychology?

Key terms
biopsychology, reductionism, physiology, emergent properties, physiological psychology

Significant psychologists
James, Hebb, Lashley

Revision questions
- What do biopsychologists investigate?
- What is physiological reductionism? Describe two weaknesses of a reductionist approach to biopsychology.
- What do you understand by the term "emergent properties"?
- How has animal research changed over the past three decades?
- Give three examples of practical applications of animal research in physiological psychology.

The nervous system

Key terms
neurone, synapse, central nervous system, autonomic nervous system, cerebral cortex

Significant figures
Berger, Moniz, MacLean, Phineas Gage

Revision questions
- Briefly describe how nerve cells transmit information around the body.
- What are the main types of neurone, and what functions do they serve?
- What role do neurotransmitters play in the nervous system?
- Distinguish between intrusive and non-intrusive methods of studying the brain's functioning.
- What are the major areas of localised function on the cerebral cortex?

Language, hemisphere function & memory

Key terms
cerebro-vascular disorders, aphasia, dyslexia, split-brain studies, bilateral, retrograde amnesia

Significant psychologists
Broca, Wernicke, Sperry, Annett, Geshwind, Lashley

Revision questions
- What are the areas of the brain involved in processing language?
- What have split-brain studies told us about hemisphere functioning?
- Describe two techniques other than split-brain studies, which have been used to study hemisphere functioning.
- What different types of amnesia are there?
- What neural effects does Alzheimer's disease produce?

Stress, anxiety & emotion

Key terms
stress, coping, fight or flight, General Adaptation Syndrome, James–Lange theory, cognitive appraisal

Significant psychologists
Selye, Frankenhaeuser, Friedman and Rosenman, Schachter and Singer

Revision questions
- Briefly distinguish between the two divisions of the autonomic nervous system.
- What are the main physiological processes involved in the fight or flight response?
- How has drug research helped us to understand the physiological mechanisms of anxiety?
- What structures of the brain appear to be involved in emotional experience?
- What are the two main approaches to the role of cognitive appraisal in emotion?

Sleep, arousal & motivation

Key terms
The Yerkes–Dodson Law, psychophysiology, arousal, biological rhythm, REM sleep, homoeostasis, set-weight, satiation

Significant psychologists
Kleitman, Dement, Oswald, Nisbett, Olds and Milner

Revision questions
- Describe which two different kinds of arousal have been measured by psychologists.
- Outline the internal and external factors involved in jet-lag, and suggest ways in which jet-lag can be reduced.
- What electrical and chemical activity in the brain is associated with sleep and dreaming?
- What role does the ventro-medial nucleus of the hypothalamus play in controlling hunger?
- What are the two main types of thirst, and how do they differ physiologically?

Sensory information processing

Key terms
transduction, somatosensory, olfaction, proprioception, receptive field, orientation column, blindsight

Significant psychologists
Melzack, Helmholtz, Hubel and Wiesel, Blakemore

Revision questions
- What does the information which reaches the somatosensory cortex describe?
- Briefly outline the gate control theory of pain.

- How is the sense of smell different from the other senses?
- Describe the structure of the retina, and explain how it processes light information.
- Briefly outline how shape is processed in the visual system.

COMPARATIVE PSYCHOLOGY

Comparative psychology & evolution

Key terms
comparative psychology, evolution, biodiversity, *Zeitgeist*, sociobiology, coevolution

Significant psychologists
Darwin, Lloyd Morgan, E. O. Wilson

Revision questions
- How useful is Cartesian dualism for our understanding of animals?
- Illustrate the concept of levels of explanation by showing its relevance for a specific example of animal activity.
- Outline and evaluate the concept of the phylogenetic scale.
- Describe Tinbergen's four areas of comparative psychology, giving a practical example of each one.
- Outline and briefly discuss three different versions of evolutionary theory.

The basis of behaviour

Key terms
genetics, fixed action patterns, sign stimuli, innate releasing mechanisms, operant conditioning, classical conditioning, learning sets

Significant psychologists
Lorenz, Skinner, Seligman

Revision questions
- How can the process of meiosis influence inherited behaviour?
- Briefly outline the defining characteristics of inherited behaviour.
- What is a fixed action pattern, and how does it become manifest in an animal's behaviour?
- Describe Hailman's study of instinctive behaviour, and discuss its implications.
- Describe the basic processes of classical and operant conditioning.

Courtship, mating, & reproduction

Key terms
courtship rituals, pair-bonding, parenting, imprinting, attachment

Significant psychologists
Tinbergen, Hess, Harlow

Revision questions
- Compare and contrast two different theories of courtship behaviour.
- Describe a study illustrating co-operation in courtship behaviour.
- What are the main phases of maternal behaviour in rhesus monkeys?
- What are the significant features of imprinting?
- What were the long-term effects of bringing up young monkeys in isolation from their own kind?

Social organisation

Key terms
territoriality, frustration–aggression, game theory, anti-predator behaviour, dominance, reconciliation

Significant psychologists
Wynne-Edwards, Rowell, de Waal

Revision questions
- Describe one study of aggression in animals, and discuss its implications.
- Briefly outline the main comparative explanations for aggression.
- Distinguish between different forms of territoriality, giving for each an example of an animal species which adopts that form of behaviour.
- Describe three examples of anti-predator behaviour drawn from comparative research.
- Discuss the implication of Rowell's study of dominance structures in baboon societies.

Communication & information

Key terms
communication, electromagnetic radiation, infrasound, ultrasound, pheromone, ontogeny

Significant psychologists
Marler, von Frisch, Cheyney and Seyfarth

Revision questions
- Outline the major definitions of animal communication, giving an example of each one.
- What did Narins and Capranica discover about the calls of Puerto Rican tree frogs?
- How do honey bees signal the location of food to other hive members?
- What are pheromones, and how can they affect animal behaviour?
- Describe and evaluate two studies of animal "words".

Animal cognition

Key terms
imitation, cognitive maps, homing, Ameslan, design features, genetic preparedness

Significant psychologists
Tolman, Savage-Rumbaugh, Gould

Revision questions
- Describe one study of imitation in birds.
- Describe and discuss the evidence for the existence of cognitive maps in rats.
- How do pigeons "home"?
- Compare two studies of novel behaviour in animals.
- Evaluate the evidence for and against non-human animals having self-concepts.

7

Teaching schemes

INTRODUCTION

In this chapter, we have provided ideas for teaching schemes, which should help new lecturers and teachers to plan how they will go about teaching introductory psychology. Even at introductory level, the subject is vast, of course, and there is a great deal to cover. But different courses allow very different amounts of time for teaching introductory psychology. We have tried to allow for three eventualities, ranging from the lecturer with plenty of time to cover each part of the syllabus, to the lecturer who is trying to "squeeze a quart into a pint pot".

Like the rest of this book, our teaching schemes are organised in modular form, since introductory psychology is so often taught as a series of modules. The exception to this, though, is the area known as "perspectives", which is normally integrated with other topics as occasions arise. We begin the chapter with a discussion of how perspectives can be taught, and give examples of topics which can be used to highlight various issues. Following that, the rest of the chapter continues with the three main teaching schemes. These teaching schemes cover three different eventualities, ranging from the "deluxe" option of having twelve or more weeks to cover each of the main areas of psychology, to the rather cramped option of having to cover a whole area in just four weeks.

HOW TO TEACH PERSPECTIVES

General perspectives

Perspectives can be one of the most interesting and challenging aspects of studying psychology. Unfortunately many students often find it disorienting, since it doesn't seem to fit conveniently into standard ideas about information-to-be-learned.

It is often useful to think of perspectives in terms of different kinds of lenses that can be looked through. Each lens will reveal different concepts or ideas, and highlight the outcomes of differing underlying assumptions.

Therefore the study of perspectives actually requires students to take an overview of the discipline; to look at it from the top down, ignoring the small details and focusing on the ebb and flow of different kinds of ideas and themes.

For this reason there is a controversy as to whether one should start the course by teaching perspectives, and thereby giving students a framework within which to view psychology; or whether it makes more sense for perspectives to be taught at the end of the course when students can use their own knowledge of the subject to aid their understanding of the key debates. Whichever view you hold, it is evident that questions about perspectives can be raised throughout the course.

Schools of thought	Debates
Psychoanalysis	Freedom versus determinism
Behaviourism	Nature versus nurture
Gestalt psychology	Reductionism/levels of explanation
Humanistic psychology	Mind/body (dualism)
The "cognitive revolution"	Psychology as a science

Issues	Methods
Ethics	Ideographic/nomothetic/hermeneutic
Animal research	Causal/correlational methods
Social control	Ecological validity

While there are always overlaps, the major perspectives can be categorised into four "sets", roughly as shown in the diagram above.

As you can see, each "set" is dealing with a different type of concern. They won't be relevant for every single topic, of course, but as a general rule, you will find that every area of psychology has something to contribute to our understanding of each of these "sets".

In the rest of this section we will look at how you might incorporate some of the main issues in perspectives into your teaching, as you cover the various areas of psychology. The different themes come up several times, and in several different ways. The lists below give examples of topics which can be used to highlight different concerns. They are only intended as a beginning, and as with most aspects of perspectives, can be controversial. As you work through the themes you are bound to find many other examples, because these themes and issues permeate the whole of psychology—indeed that's why we bother to teach perspectives in the first place!

SOCIAL PSYCHOLOGY

Schools of thought
behaviourism: behavioural studies of social interaction, e.g. measures of distance and eye-contact
humanistic psychology: Maslow's theory of human needs
cognitive: social cognition, attribution

Debates
mind–body: primeval "mob" theories of crowd psychology vs. modern approaches

Issues
reductionism: social impact theory
levels of explanation: European social psychology
ethical issues: studies manipulating self-esteem; obedience etc.

Methods
nomothetic: studies of normative behaviour, e.g. conformity
hermeneutic: studies of lay beliefs and social representations; discourse analysis

COGNITIVE PSYCHOLOGY

Schools of thought
behaviourism: S-R theories of pattern recognition
Gestalt: insight learning; Gestalt laws of perception
cognitive: almost everything, really, but particularly developments in memory theory (e.g. working memory)

Debates
mind–body: hypnosis and memory; state-dependent memory

Issues
levels of explanation: bottom-up and top-down theories of perception (e.g. Gibson/Gregory)
ethical issues: studies of subliminal perception

Methods
ecological validity: studies of word recognition; studying memory using nonsense syllables
causal/correlational studies: laboratory memory studies; diary methods of investigating memory failures

BIOPSYCHOLOGY

Schools of thought
behaviourism: studies of motivation; ESB
psychoanalysis: theories of dreaming
cognitive: cognitive dimensions of stress and arousal; theories of emotion; dreaming

Debates
mind–body: Schachter's theory of emotion

Issues
determinism: the James–Lange theory of emotion (physiological determinism)
ethical issues: animal studies of brain functioning; double-blind controls and deception in drug studies

Methods
idiographic: use of case studies to investigate brain functioning
correlational studies: accidental injury and behavioural/cognitive disorders

INDIVIDUAL DIFFERENCES

Schools of thought
psychoanalysis: psychoanalytic theory; approaches to psychoanalysis
behaviourism: S-R models of personality; behaviour therapy/modification
Gestalt: Gestalt therapy
humanism: Rogerian therapy; anti-psychiatry
cognitive: Cognitive therapy; attributional aspects of depression etc.

Debates
nature–nurture: causes of intelligence; personality traits

Issues
determinism: Eysenck's theory of personality
ethical issues: effectiveness of psychoanalysis; bias in IQ tests

Methods
idiographic: e.g. Freudian theory
nomothetic: e.g. Eysenck's trait theory
hermeneutic/phenomenological: e.g. Rogers' personality theory

DEVELOPMENTAL PSYCHOLOGY

Schools of thought
psychoanalysis: Freud's theory of child personality development
behaviourism: Skinner's theory of language development
cognitive: child's theory of mind; Piagetian perspectives

Debates
nature–nurture: language acquisition

Issues
determinism: genetic/biological/conditioning models of child development
ethical issues: Freudian theory and child sexual abuse; psychoanalysis and personal privacy

Methods
ecological validity: Piagetian studies
causal/correlational: experiments on child's theory of mind/observational studies of play

COMPARATIVE PSYCHOLOGY

Schools of thought
behaviourism: classical and operant conditioning
Gestalt: insight learning
cognitive: preparedness in learning/ "learning by instinct"; animal communication

Debates
nature–nurture: studies of animal language and "culture"; sociobiology vs. biodiversity

Issues
determinism: biological determinants of behaviour, e.g. sociobiology, Lorenz's theory of human aggression

ethical issues: animal studies of crowding; training animals for military purposes

Methods
causal/correlational: animal experimentation vs. ethological studies of animal behaviour
ecological validity: laboratory studies of animal learning

THREE TEACHING SCHEMES

These teaching schemes are based on the assumption that you have at least a couple of sessions a week with your class or seminar group, and so for the most part each week's programme falls naturally into two parts. But there are other ways of dividing them up, and you need to choose the ones which suit you. These are not intended as a set of absolute instructions, but as a guide, to show you how you might organise the material. Feel free to use them if you find them helpful; ignore them if you don't.

TEACHING FULL-LENGTH MODULES

This set of teaching schemes assumes that you have a full 12 weeks, or a whole semester, to cover each of the modules in your introductory psychology course. Having a whole term or even more means that you will be able to go into each topic in some depth, and bring out its nuances and implications fully. If you find that you have even more teaching time for the module than our plans allow, you can fill in extra weeks with revision or assessment activities; or with some kind of additional "learning experience" (like a visit or talk from an external speaker) which will help your students to appreciate some of the broader implications of what they are learning.

Cognitive Psychology

Week 1
Introduction to cognition: what is cognitive psychology? Cognition in the real world.

Week 2
Sensory information processing: vision, hearing, sensory thresholds and psychophysics. Perceptual development.

Week 3
Perceptual organisation: Gestalt principles; constancies, illusions. Perceiving depth, movement and patterns. Theories of perception.

Week 4
The process of attention: selective and focused attention. Theories of selective attention. Divided attention and influencing factors.

Week 5
Automatic processing and absent-mindedness. Methods of studying attention. Vigilance (sustained attention).

Week 6
Organisation of memory: stores, semantic memory and schemata. Short-term and long-term memory; levels of processing.

Week 7
Theories of forgetting. Practical applications of research. Methods of studying memory processes. Applying memory theory to revising.

Week 8
Language production: the differences between speech and writing. Language comprehension: mechanisms, contexts, schemata and inference.

Week 9
The relationship between language and thinking. Reading: basic mechanisms and the influence of contexts.

Week 10
Problem solving: set, fixedness, and other effects of experience. Computer simulation and artificial intelligence.

Week 11
Deductive reasoning and concept-formation. Heuristics involved in decision making and judgement.

Week 12
Perspectives in cognitive psychology: top-down and bottom-up theories, the computer metaphor. Information processing. Examples of each of these drawn from the material studied. Ethical issues in cognitive research.

Social Psychology

Week 1
Introduction to social psychology: basic concepts, cultural aspects of self.

Week 2
Methods of study in social psychology. Self-fulfilling prophecies and demand characteristics.

Week 3
Non-verbal communication.

Week 4
Attribution, explanation and social representations.

Week 5
Audience effects and bystanders. Social impact theory.

Week 6
Conformity and obedience.

Week 7
Groups and leadership.

Week 8
Person perception and impression formation.

Week 9
Attraction and relationships.

Week 10
Attitudes and persuasion.

Week 11
Prejudice and prejudice reduction.

Week 12
Aggression, altruism and collective behaviour.

Developmental Psychology

Week 1
Origins and principles of developmental psychology.

Week 2
Pre-natal development and attachment.

Week 3
Infant perception.

Week 4
Skills and knowledge in infancy.

Week 5
Early childhood: cognitive development and language.

Week 6
Early childhood: play and social development.

Week 7
Middle childhood: cognitive and moral development.

Week 8
Middle childhood: school, literacy and numeracy.

Week 9
Adolescence: cognitive development.

Week 10
Adolescence: social and moral development.

Week 11
Adulthood and lifespan development.

Week 12
Ageing and retirement.

Individual Differences

Week 1
Introduction to individual differences: individual differences in the real world.

Week 2
Defining intelligence. Intelligence testing. The nature–nurture debate on intelligence.

Week 3
Factor theories of intelligence. Contemporary theories.

Week 4
Measuring personality. Type and trait approaches in personality assessment.

Week 5
Factor theories of personality. Situationism, interactionism and social constructivism.

Week 6
Cognitive theories of personality: personal construct theory.

Week 7
Rogers' phenomenological theory, social cognitive theory.

Week 8
Defining abnormality. Classificatory systems of psychiatric disorder.

Week 9
Explaining mental disorders: behavioural, medical and psychoanalytic models.

Week 10
Specific psychiatric disorders: schizophrenia, depression etc.

Week 11
Therapeutic approaches: behaviour therapy; psychotherapy; cognitive therapy.

Week 12
Forms of somatic therapy; evaluation of therapeutic effectiveness.

Biopsychology

Week 1
Introduction to physiological psychology; physiological psychology in the real world.

Week 2
The nervous system.

Week 3
Organisation of the nervous system.

Week 4
Language.

Week 5
Hemisphere function.

Week 6
Learning and memory.

Week 7
Stress, anxiety and emotion.

Week 8
Sleep, arousal and biological rhythms.

Week 9
Motivation.

Week 10
Sensory systems.

Week 11
The visual system.

Week 12
Perspectives in biopsychology: ethics, reductionism, methods of study.

Comparative Psychology

Week 1
Introduction to comparative psychology: history and fundamental concepts. Popularised versions of comparative psychology.

Week 2
The theory of evolution. Versions of evolutionary theory.

Week 3
Mechanisms of genetic transmission. Inherited behaviour.

Week 4
Mechanisms of conditioning. Critical and sensitive periods.

Week 5
Courtship and mating. Theories of courtship.

Week 6
Parental behaviour, imprinting and attachment.

Week 7
Territoriality and aggression. Anti-predator behaviour.

Week 8
Forms of social organisation. Reconciliation and peace-making.

Week 9
Animal sense reception: sensory modes.

Week 10
Animal communication in the wild.

Week 11
Teaching non-human animals to use language.

Week 12
Studies of animal cognition. Evolutionary perspectives on animal learning.

THE 8-WEEK MODULES

This set of teaching schemes assumes that you have eight weeks or so for teaching each module in your introductory course, perhaps including a couple of classes or lectures each week. It is a little more streamlined than the deluxe model outlined above, sticking more rigorously to the main topics involved in conventional introductory syllabuses, and leaving out a few of the newer or broader topics. Even so, it will provide students with a reasonable groundwork for further study, and should give them a thorough understanding of the main, or "core" topics in each area of psychology.

Cognitive Psychology

Week 1
Introduction to cognition: what is cognitive psychology? Sensation and perception: sensory information processing.

Week 2
Perceptual organisation and perceptual development. The nature–nurture debate in perception.

Week 3
Theories of perception. Top-down and bottom-up theories in cognitive psychology. Theories of selective attention.

Week 4
Organising memory: stores, semantic memory and schemata. The two-process theory of memory vs. levels of processing theory.

Week 5
Theories of forgetting. Practical applications of memory research. Everyday memory and the study of memory processes. Applying memory theory to revising for exams.

Week 6
Problem solving: set, fixedness, and other effects of experience. Computer simulation and artificial intelligence.

Week 7
The relationship between language and thought. The production and comprehension of language.

Week 8
Methods of studying cognitive psychology. Perspectives in cognitive psychology: top-down and bottom-up theories, the computer metaphor, ethical issues.

Social Psychology

Week 1
Concepts and methods in social psychology.

Week 2
Non-verbal communication.

Week 3
Conformity and obedience.

Week 4
Audience effects, bystanders and group behaviour.

Week 5
Attribution, explanation and social representations.

Week 6
Person perception and attraction.

Week 7
Attitudes and prejudice.

Week 8
Aggression, altruism and collective behaviour.

Developmental Psychology

Week 1
Origins and principles of developmental psychology.

Week 2
Infant perception and pre-natal development.

Week 3
Skills and knowledge in infancy. Attachment.

Week 4
Early childhood: cognitive development and language.

Week 5
Early childhood: play and social development.

Week 6
Middle childhood: cognitive and moral development, schooling.

Week 7
Adolescence.

Week 8
Adulthood and ageing.

Individual Differences

Week 1
Introduction to individual differences. Reliability in personality and intelligence.

Week 2
Theories of intelligence: factor theories and contemporary approaches.

Week 3
IQ testing and the nature–nurture debate in intelligence.

Week 4
Personality assessment; trait theories of personality.

Week 5
Cognitive approaches to personality: personal constructions, phenomenology, social cognition.

Week 6
The medical model. Classifying psychiatric disorders. Specific disorders.

Week 7
Alternatives to the medical model: behavioural, psychoanalytic and cognitive models.

Week 8
Forms of therapy and their effectiveness.

Biopsychology

Week 1
Introduction to biopsychology; organisation of the nervous system.

Week 2
Neurones, synapses and neurotransmitters.

Week 3
Language and hemisphere function.

Week 4
Stress, anxiety and emotion.

Week 5
Sleep, arousal and biological rhythms.

Week 6
Motivation.

Week 7
Sensory systems including vision.

Week 8
Learning and memory; perspectives in biopsychology: ethics, reductionism, methods of study.

Comparative Psychology

Week 1
Introduction to comparative psychology. Evolution.

Week 2
Genetic transmission, conditioning, sensitive and critical periods.

Week 3
Courtship and mating. Mechanisms of inherited behaviour.

Week 4
Parental behaviour, imprinting and attachment.

Week 5
Territoriality and aggression. Anti-predatory behaviour.

Week 6
Forms of social organisation, reconciliation.

Week 7
Animal communication in the wild.

Week 8
Teaching animals to use language.

THE 24-WEEK INTRODUCTORY COURSE

This set of teaching schemes assumes that you are having to cover the whole of introductory psychology in a very limited time, having just 24 teaching weeks to go through the lot. This type of approach isn't suitable for A level psychology, obviously, which needs more depth of coverage if students are to be able to tackle their exam effectively. It can sometimes be appropriate for first-year degree courses, though, since the students sometimes only need a brief introduction because they will be taking up each topic in more detail in subsequent years. It is possible, too, that some ideas from this teaching scheme may be valuable for teachers who would normally take longer to cover a topic, but whose teaching time has been unexpectedly cut short, for one reason or another.

For each of the areas of introductory psychology covered by this scheme, we have highlighted the four major, or "core" topics, which would need to be dealt with in lectures or class; but we have also highlighted four more topics which the students should become acquainted with. These additional topics can be dealt with through structured assignments which the students can tackle in their private study time; or by using them as the focus for seminar activities or discussions.

Cognitive Psychology

Week 1
The difference between sensation and perception. Visual information processing. Perceptual organisation.

Structured assignment/seminar topic
Outline three filter models of selective attention, and describe two studies pertinent to each one.

Week 2
The nature–nurture debate on perception. Theories of perception.

Structured assignment/seminar topic
Outline the key theories of the relationship between language and thought. List two points of evidence for each one.

Week 3
Memory organisation and types of remembering. Theories of forgetting.

Structured assignment/seminar topic
List the key features of human problem solving, and the key features of research into computer simulation. Contrast the two.

Week 4
The two-process model of memory vs. levels of processing theory. Key perspectives in cognitive psychology: top-down and bottom-up theories, the computer metaphor.

Structured assignment/seminar topic
Go back over the various cognitive studies evaluating each one in terms of ethical issues.

Social Psychology

Week 5
Introduction to social psychology. Non-verbal communication.

Structured assignment/seminar topic
Audience effects.

Week 6
Conformity and obedience.

Structured assignment/seminar topic
Theories of aggression and altruism.

Week 7
Person perception and attribution.

Structured assignment/seminar topic
Bystander intervention.

Week 8
Attitudes and prejudice.

Structured assignment/seminar topic
Persuasion.

Developmental Psychology

Week 9
Introduction to developmental psychology; attachment.

Structured assignment/seminar topic
Infant perception.

Week 10
Language and social development in early childhood.

Structured assignment/seminar topic
Cognitive development.

Week 11
Cognitive development in middle childhood.

Structured assignment/seminar topic
Literacy and numeracy.

Week 12
Adulthood and ageing.

Structured assignment/seminar topic
Adolescence.

Individual Differences

Week 13
Intelligence testing; theories of intelligence.

Structured assignment/seminar topic
The nature–nurture debate on intelligence.

Week 14
Three contrasting models of personality: traits, personal constructs, Rogers.

Structured assignment/seminar topic
Measuring personality.

Week 15
Alternative models of mental disorder: medical, behavioural and psychoanalytic explanations.

Structured assignment/seminar topic
Psychiatric classification systems.

Week 16
Therapeutic approaches: behaviour therapy, psychotherapy, cognitive therapy.

Structured assignment/seminar topic
Schizophrenia and depression.

Biopsychology

Week 17
Interaction of central and autonomic nervous systems and endocrine systems. Neurones and neurotransmitters.

Structured assignment/seminar topic
The effects of drugs.

Week 18
Sleep and dreaming.

Structured assignment/seminar topic
Methods of study in biopsychology.

Week 19
Emotion, arousal and stress.

Structured assignment/seminar topic
Coping mechanisms for long-term stress.

Week 20
Motivation.

Structured assignment/seminar topic
Ethics and methods of study in biopsychology.

Comparative Psychology

Week 21
Inherited behaviour, genetics and learning.

Structured assignment/seminar topic
The theory of evolution.

Week 22
Maternal behaviour, imprinting and attachment.

Structured assignment/seminar topic
Courtship rituals.

Week 23
Territoriality, aggression and social organisation.

Structured assignment/seminar topic
Forms of territoriality.

Week 24
Teaching animals human languages.

Structured assignment/seminar topic
Bee dances and birdsong.

A note on the assignments or seminar topics:
Here, we have only outlined the possible content of the structured assignments. It's up to you exactly how you structure them, but if your students are having to work on their own from textbooks, the more you can get them to look for smallish chunks of information the better. Handing them a blank chart for them to fill in, or something similar, can be very helpful indeed. Also, you don't necessarily have to mark them: it's often a useful revision exercise to get groups of students to look at each other's, for instance. (Although they won't do it if they think you're not even interested, of course!)

Index